Public Private Partnerships

Veronica Vecchi
Francesca Casalini • Niccolò Cusumano
Velia M. Leone

Public Private Partnerships

Principles for Sustainable Contracts

palgrave
macmillan

Veronica Vecchi
School of Management - SDA Bocconi
Bocconi University
Milan, Italy

Francesca Casalini
School of Management - SDA Bocconi
Bocconi University
Milan, Italy

Niccolò Cusumano
School of Management - SDA Bocconi
Bocconi University
Milan, Italy

Velia M. Leone
Studio Legale Leone & Associati
Rome, Italy

ISBN 978-3-030-65434-4 ISBN 978-3-030-65435-1 (eBook)
https://doi.org/10.1007/978-3-030-65435-1

This Palgrave Macmillan imprint is published by the registered company Springer Nature Switzerland AG.
The registered company address is: Gewerbestrasse 11, 6330 Cham, Switzerland

To my Mum, who is an example of commitment and strength, Veronica
To Angelo, who always keeps his words, Francesca
To Veronica and Manuela, who taught me how to learn, Niccolò
To my parents—no words will ever be enough, Velia

Preface

This book has been conceived for professionals, working for public authorities, corporates, financial investors and development banks, and MSc and executive students in order to offer a broad and practical yet concise perspective on public-private partnerships (PPPs), for infrastructure development and service delivery.

Over the last 20 years, PPP has been playing a crucial role worldwide in the matching of public and private resources to close the infrastructure gap and to bring innovation to the way public services are delivered. However, it is in the aftermath of Covid-19 that PPP can play an even more strategic role. On the one hand, public debt has massively increased, thus making the involvement of private capital a priority; on the other hand, the urgency to boost GDP and employment and tackle social issues calls for a renewed use of PPP. Indeed, PPP offers not only macroeconomic benefits; it can also be a way to stimulate innovation, thanks to the know-how of economic operators and the nature of the contract (whose main feature is balanced risk allocation between authorities and private players). The latter, however, has remained in the background so far.

Today, we are not only tending to the extraordinary challenges raised by Covid-19, but also witnessing the unprecedented commitment of industrial and financial investors toward public value generation. Therefore, it is urgent and fundamental to learn how PPPs can be designed and implemented to support economic and social recovery.

A PPP is a complex contract and it has been applied so far with mixed results. In the public and private sectors, competencies are key to understanding and overcoming the weaknesses experienced so far and to approaching PPP with a different, long-term, value co-creation perspective. Until the end of 2019, PPP was seen just as a way to develop infrastructures in contexts with limited budgets. In the aftermath of Covid-19, it is no longer just a matter of mixing public and private capitals; there is now the need for a co-evolution of the public and private sector, to find joint solutions to a changed world.

This book has been written in order to support this co-evolution and, as a first step to triggering and developing it, a common background of essential principles is required.

This book mainly provides principles, based on the academic and professional experience of the authors, that have to be tailored in order to be applied across sectors and jurisdictions. PPP works well when a contract is designed on the basis of the specific needs and contexts. We refrain from standard solutions and a "me-too" approach, which did not work in the past. To share essential principles, we chose Palgrave Pivot, whose format is ideal to spread the essentials of a topic, thus making them accessible to practitioners (managers and policy makers).

We do hope readers can find in this book not only an opportunity to learn but also the inspiration to approach PPP with such a different perspective.

Milan, Italy — Veronica Vecchi
Francesca Casalini
Niccolò Cusumano
Rome, Italy — Velia M. Leone

Contents

About the Authors

Francesca Casalini, Msc is Junior Lecturer of Government Health and Not-for-Profit at SDA Bocconi School of Management and PhD candidate and research assistant at the Institute of Systemic Governance and Public Management, University of St. Gallen. Her areas of expertise include business modeling in multiple sectors (both for-profit and not-for-profit), public-private partnerships, ecosystems, and platform-based collaborations. Francesca has been research grantee of the European Investment Bank and the Asian Development Bank on the topic of infrastructure financing. She has served as advisor of several public authorities and economic operators to assess the financial viability of PPP transactions.

Niccolò Cusumano, PhD is Associate Professor of Practice of Government, Health and Not-for-Profit at SDA Bocconi School of Management. Contract professor at Bocconi University, Niccolò teaches in courses of Economics and Management of Public Institutions and Non-Profit Organization and Project Management & Funding of International Programs. From 2017, he coordinates the advanced course in Health Contracting and Purchasing Management (MASAN). His research activity focuses on public-private interactions, in particular in the context of public contracts, and PPP. Another stream of research focuses on sustainability: renewable energy sources, energy efficiency policies for which he has participated in numerous researches and written scientific papers.

Velia M. Leone, LLM is founding partner of Leone & Associati Law Firm, after being the resident partner of a London-based law firm in Brussels and serving as Chief Legal Counsel at the Italian PPP Task Force. She has an outstanding experience of over 25 years in the field of PPP. She is one of the leading experts at national level and very well known internationally as a reference in matters relating to PPP and public procurement. On these topics she advices private and public clients, at national and international level. A much-appreciated lecturer, she has formerly been teaching at the European Institute of Public Administration in Maastricht, University of Tor Vergata, University of Trento, and National School of Public Administration. She is SDA Bocconi School of Management fellow.

Veronica Vecchi, PhD is Associate Professor of Practice of Government Health and Not-for-Profit at SDA Bocconi School of Management, where she teaches and conducts research on public-private collaborations, infrastructure financing, long-term investment, impact investing, and public procurement. She teaches Financial Management in Governments and International Organizations and Long-Term Investments & PPP at the Bocconi University. She serves as director of Executive Education at SDA Bocconi Asia Center, in Mumbai, India, where she is also the director of the International Executive Master in Business. She is advisor of several public authorities, market players, and development banks on PPP. She is Board Member of Italgas, an Italian listed company, which is one of the largest European player in gas distribution, where she is also member of sustainability committee. She also serves as member of the Academic Advisory Board of the Global Infrastructure Hub—a G20 initiative.

List of Figures

List of Boxes

List of Tables

CHAPTER 1

Public-Private Partnerships for Infrastructure and Service Delivery: An Introduction

Veronica Vecchi, Francesca Casalini, Niccolò Cusumano, and Velia M. Leone

Abstract This chapter provides a wide framework to understand how public and private actors collaborate. Collaborations happen at three different levels (macro, meso, and micro) and with different levels of intensity and formalization. Despite the mixed results experienced so far with public-private partnerships (PPPs) for infrastructure and service delivery, the shift toward a new approach to sustainability by corporations can certainly prove useful to reconceive the way in which PPP is used and structured. Further, Covid-19 pandemic has shed a new light on the importance of collaborations to improve resilience and foster innovation. This chapter also presents the main feature of PPP contracts for infrastructure and service delivery, which are the focus of this book; the policy goals that could be pursued and the main challenges to achieve such goals.

Keywords Public-private collaborations • Public value • Public procurement • Economic and social infrastructures • Benefits and drawbacks of PPP

V. Vecchi et al., *Public Private Partnerships*,
https://doi.org/10.1007/978-3-030-65435-1_1

1.1 Public-Private Collaborations in General: A Comprehensive Framework

This book is about public-private partnerships (hereafter, PPPs) for infrastructure development and/or service delivery. PPPs, as a first approximation, may be understood as a formalized cooperation between the public and the private sector, based on mutual trust and shared goals such as stepping up quality standards and sustainability for the provision of services and infrastructures.

PPPs, for instance, encompass a wide array of cooperating forms. In this chapter we will provide an overview of different kinds of PPPs, in their wider understanding, and, then, focus on the most specific features of PPP contracts, their peculiarities, their possible evolution, and their strategic use toward the achievement of wider policy goals.

PPP is often associated with bundled contracts for financing, building, and operating an infrastructure—or even for service delivery and, therefore, without involving a major investment component. These kinds of partnerships can be considered as having a contractual nature, since the partnership is established through a (mid/long-term) contract between the competent public, or contracting authority (hereafter, CA), and the economic operator (hereafter, EO). Nevertheless, other forms of collaboration between the public and the private sectors exist and they have been increasingly important since the 2008 global economic and financial crisis and, furthermore, in the aftermath of the Covid-19 pandemic.

Figure 1.1 shows a conceptual scheme useful for understanding the main types of public-private collaborations.

Collaborations may be developed on three levels: macro, meso, and micro. Starting from the bottom of the scheme, at *macro level*, collaborations are informal and mainly intended to influence policy design. Further, at this level, informal collaborations can be originated from corporates' sustainability strategies. Since more and more companies reject the idea of pure profit maximization and feel an obligation to contribute to the solution of societal challenges—which they may have contributed to create in the past with wrong business practices—they are willing to act as responsible partners and advocate for innovative solutions to create social value (Hartley et al. 2013). Stakeholder theory (Freeman et al. 2010; Jensen 2010), Corporate Social Responsibility (CSR) theory (Carroll 1979, 1991; Garriga and Melé 2004), and its strategic approach (Baron 2001; Bhattacharyya 2010; McElhaney 2009; Porter and Kramer 2006) lately evolved into shared value (Porter and Kramer 2006, 2011), underpin

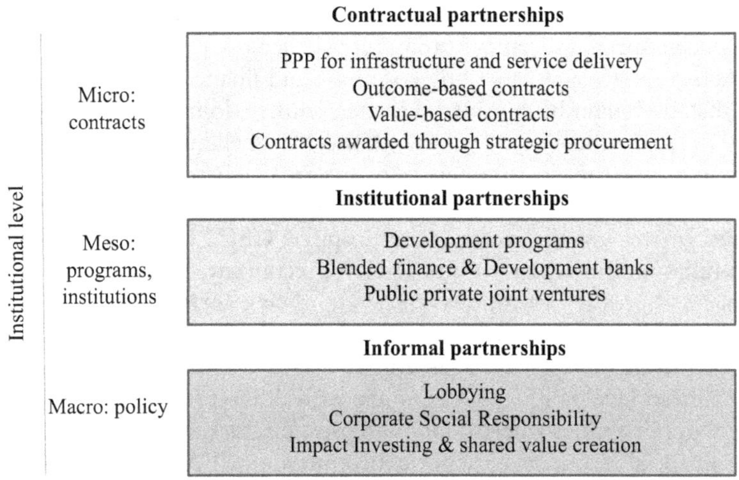

Fig. 1.1 Forms of public-private collaborations. Source: Authors

from a theoretical perspective such efforts. Within responsibility agendas, corporations contribute to generate public and shared value: in other words, they proactively incorporate the pursuit of some societal goals in their strategies, thus behaving as responsible corporate citizens. For some companies, CSR is becoming a strategic component of their competitive advantage and a way to attract responsible investors, that is, those including Environmental, Social, and Governance (ESG) criteria in their investment decisions. Michael Porter captured these trends with the conceptualization of the social dimension of the competitive advantage (Porter and Kramer 2006) and, later, with the shared value creation (Porter and Kramer 2011) sustains that societal challenges can represent a new business field in which it is possible to create profit while achieving social value.

Balancing financial and social return is also a new investment approach, which takes the name of impact investing and is attracting more and more investors. More in general, according to the Global Sustainable Investment Alliance (2018),[1] sustainable investments are growing, and they include not only the so-called negative/exclusionary screening ones—in other words, those excluding certain harmful sectors—but also, where the main

[1] http://www.gsi-alliance.org/wp-content/uploads/2019/06/GSIR_Review2018F.pdf

increase is recorded, those that integrate ESG dimensions or even those that tackle specific social or community challenges.

According to such emerging corporate and financial perspectives, society shall no longer be considered as the exclusive domain of public authorities or philanthropists. Social and societal challenges (such as global warming and the environment) are a terrain where public and private actors can work together (collaborate) to generate what is called public value. In the last few years, many inspired CEOs have expressed their strong commitment to a purpose-driven economy, trying to encourage public and private institutions to scale up their efforts. When public policies are designed to incentivize such efforts, an innovative form of macro public-private collaboration can ensue.

At **meso level**, PPP collaborations, with different degrees of intensity, create opportunities where public and private actors combine financial and non-financial resources to achieve a common goal. At this level, we find, on one hand, institutional partnerships, such as public-private-owned companies/joint-ventures (where the partnership is institutionalized through the setting up of a legal entity); on the other hand, programs that have been co-designed and are co-implemented by public and private bodies to achieve social and economic development goals. These programs can be co-funded or they can mobilize individual investments toward such mutual goals. The level of formalization of such programs may significantly vary; for example, they can be implemented through associations or memorandums of understanding. Development banks are among the key actors at this level. They operate at regional, national, or supra-national level and can also be set up through different models of public-private governance. A relevant example of meso collaboration is represented by blended finance programs, aimed at attracting (or crowding-in) traditional investors in riskier investments, such as impact investing or PPP initiatives, especially in emerging countries, as discussed in Chap. 2.

At **micro level**, PPP is a contract entered into by two parties, that is, the CA and the EO. These contracts—which are the main focus of this book—have a mid/long-term horizon and they allocate risks between the two parties in order to create incentives to achieve complex and/or innovative goals, which are more difficult to achieve through a traditional public procurement contract. The objective of such contract is usually the delivery of a service or the development and operation of an infrastructure where the EO is paid based on the results achieved, according to different contract schemes, discussed in Chap. 4. Concisely, such payments can be either in the form of tariffs from end-users (when the EO retains the demand risk) or availability charges, paid by the CA in return for a non-core service. In this instance, CAs retain full responsibility for the delivery of the main, or core, service. In recent years, outcome-based PPP contracts (OBC), also known as Social Impact Bonds (SIBs), have emerged: here, a premium is paid to EOs in proportion to the social result/outcome achieved. SIB contracts are discussed in Chap. 6. At this level, partnerships can also be established for the delivery of goods and services through strategic public procurement. However, these contracts are often regarded as supply contracts, under a legal perspective, as explained in Chap. 3.

PPP contracts are relevant especially in strategic sectors, such as defense or healthcare. In the latter, the importance of partnership has emerged during the Covid-19 pandemic; more in general, the healthcare sector can leverage on contractual partnerships, such as value-based contracts, in order to optimize financial resources while increasing the effectiveness of purchases, such as pharmaceutical products, medical devices, medical equipment, and IT solutions.

1.2 PPP: Main Features and Applications

PPP contracts for infrastructure and service delivery, the focus of this book, are characterized by four main features:

1. Mid/long-term agreement
2. Investment of private capitals on an exclusive basis or with a co-investment of public money
3. Risk allocation between public and private parties
4. Performance-related pay (i.e. based on results or outcome).

A PPP is a long-term contract between a public authority and, usually, a special purpose vehicle (SPV), in order to design, finance, build, and operate economic or social infrastructure. The SPV is responsible for delivering associated works and services on time, on budget, and on quality. A well-drafted PPP contract is characterized by balanced risk allocation between the public authority and the SPV.

SPVs are generally set up to ring-fence project risks and cash flows, thus fostering the attraction of capitals (see Box 1.1).

Two kinds of private sponsors are involved in PPP transactions: pure financial investors, that is, those investing their capital (in the form of

Box 1.1 The role of SPV in PPP contracts

In PPP projects, SPVs are fundamental to attracting financial resources and subsequently dedicating them to the project development; further the SPV insulates the project cash flows to service the debt. Through the SPV, such resources are ring-fenced vis-à-vis the sponsors' or other shareholders' assets, therefore lenders have limited recourse to the shareholders' own assets (see Chap. 2).

This model allows EOs to engage in several investments at the same time and without risking all their assets. Furthermore, the establishment of an SPV represents a guarantee also for the CAs, because:

- the SPV's capital is dedicated solely to the performance of a specific contract, and
- the project cash flow cannot be used for a scope different than repaying lenders' financing of the investments and costs deriving from the contract, nor can risk being affected by the soundness of other activities carried out by individual EOs holding the SPV's shares.

PPP contracts may apply to a variety of projects and may take different forms, according to the nature of the infrastructure/service involved. PPP may be used for the building and operation of economic and social infrastructure, but also for service delivery in itself, resulting in a minor upfront investment.

equity and shareholder loans) in the SPV, and industrial investors. The latter generally invest money in the SPV and are entrusted by the SPV, through sub-contracts, to build the infrastructure and/or operate and manage the underlying services. Indeed, industrial players invest in the SPV's equity to expand their business and to gain access to better economic conditions for subcontracted activities. The SPV may use subcontractors different from the players that are also industrial investors. It is also widespread for industrial sponsors that are subcontractors to further subcontract part of the activities assigned by the SPV.

In sectors where PPP contracts are applied as a standard way to deliver public services, the involved EOs are, usually, large companies, often listed, who may decide not to establish an SPV.

A PPP contract is generally financed through a project finance scheme, where a large portion of the investment is financed with debt in the form of syndicated loans or bonds (see Chap. 2).

Economic infrastructures refer to, for instance, the energy, transportation, and telecommunication sectors. Typical social infrastructures are hospitals, schools, and affordable housing. Generally, economic infrastructures are paid for by their users through tariffs or fees (the acronym BOT—build, operate, and transfer—contract is often used to refer to such transactions). In social infrastructure, the remuneration of investors usually stems from an availability payment, that is, a fee paid by the competent public authority, which uses infrastructure and related services to deliver core public services. Availability contracts are also known as DBFMO, that stands for design, build, finance, maintain, and operate. Chapter 4 analyzes in detail different types of PPP contracts for economic and social infrastructure. In any event, although at international level different contract and payment schemes are used, an efficient PPP contract must be tailored based on local jurisdiction and regulatory context.

PPP contracts can be used for greenfield projects—frequently used in emerging countries—and brownfield projects—targeting already existing infrastructure to be revamped and refurbished. In the latter case, the level of risk is lower, since capital investments are lower and demand is already known and therefore more predictable.

BOT contracts are usually construed as concessions, while DBFMO contracts were introduced under the label of "public private partnership." Nowadays, this distinction is no longer relevant: however, it still creates certain confusion, since the term "concession" has a legal nature, while the term "PPP" has a more generic meaning.

From a legal perspective, the most appropriate contract type for a PPP is a concession model, as it transfers a higher level of risk to EOs, contrary to traditional procurement. In the context of EU law, this distinction is defined in the Concession Directive, according to which the distinctive feature of concessions is the transfer of operating risk to EOs, as it is explained in Chap. 3.

Figure 1.2 shows the standard structure for a PPP project.

PPP is widely regarded as a way to attract long-term investors in infrastructure development, thus contributing to the closure of the infrastructure gap. At the time of writing, the infrastructure gap is estimated by the

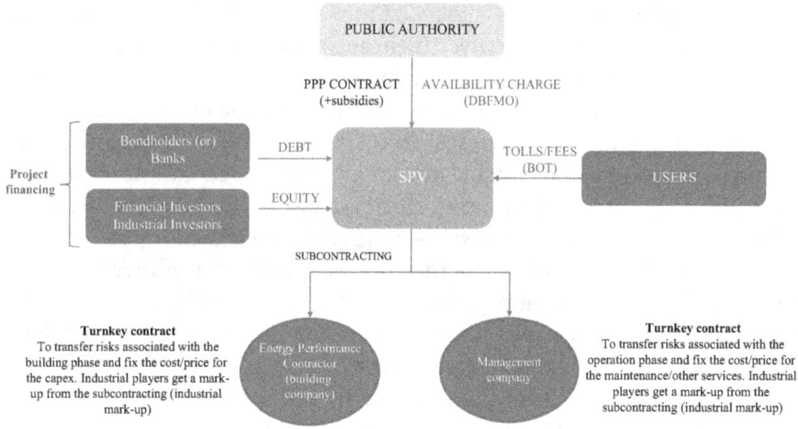

Fig. 1.2 Standard structure of a PPP project. Source: Authors

OECD, WEF, IMF, World Bank, and various academic institutions to be somewhere between \$2 trillion and \$3 trillion per year. This takes into account the dual need to modernize and expand infrastructure, as well as the need to make green investments called for by the UN sustainable development goals (SDGs).

Box 1.2 provides a definition of the infrastructure gap.

PPPs are used to involve EOs in the development or operation of infrastructure that cannot be privatized because they represent a natural monopoly, or, in some instances, for policy reasons (as described in Box 1.3). However, as stated in Sects. 1.1 and 1.4, PPP is also a way to encourage EOs to deliver more innovative public services, that is, of better quality or with a superior outcome.

Therefore, PPP is the ideal tool to attract capitals and know-how able to ensure the efficiency and effectiveness of public services. Furthermore, PPP can foster competition (for the market) even in a context of natural monopoly, such as network infrastructure.

Box 1.2 Infrastructure gap

The infrastructure gap, broadly speaking, is defined as an inadequate level of infrastructure or as the difference between investment needs and actual spending.

There are many existing estimates at local, national, regional, and world-wide level, calculated according to a variety of models that can be categorized as (1) bottom-up microeconomic or micro-engineering models, (2) top-down macroeconomic models, and (3) hybrid models.

Microeconomic and micro-engineering models are both based on bottom-up sectoral knowledge and encompass a wide variety of grey literature, from national project pipelines, which may span from a basic project list identifying local gaps, to comprehensive reports, such as the UK Infrastructure and Projects Authority Report (one of the most detailed ones in Europe), to sectoral analyses. Research on macroeconomic models, which explain and predict levels of infrastructure based on macroeconomic variables, stems from the seminal research conducted by Marianne Fay for the World Bank Group in 2000. This work disentangled the primary relationship between macroeconomic variables and the level of infrastructure needed. Finally, hybrid models are a combination of sectoral approaches to macroeconomic evaluations.

Looking at the most recent estimates, according to Global Infrastructure Hub (GIH), a G20 initiative, the infrastructure gap globally amounts to $15 trillion and $18 trillion if you also consider the investments needed to achieve sustainable development goals (SDGs). It should be noted that this value refers to "economic" infrastructures: roads, ports, airports, telecommunications, energy, and water. GIH does not therefore represent the infrastructural gap for social sectors, such as health, education, and affordable/social housing.

This is a gap estimated using an econometric model in which the future investment needs of a single country are defined as the value of the infrastructural stock necessary to ensure an economic performance equal to that of the countries deemed most competitive for a similar level of development. In other words, it is a question of comparing the situation of a country to a reference benchmark. The requirement is then weighed by "country-specific" factors (e.g. economic structure, population density) and "sector specific" factors (typical of the economic sectors considered).

Box 1.3 PPP versus privatization

It is worth clarifying that PPPs are not equivalent to privatization of infrastructure or related services. Rather, PPPs are a way to finance the development of infrastructure through private or public-private capitals, whose remuneration depends on the management of the services delivered through the underlying infrastructure.

The scientific literature distinguishes in a clear manner a partnership (i.e. a PPP) from standard outsourcing. A partnership is aimed at introducing a system of risks and rewards to create incentives to economic players to achieve challenging results, accruing remuneration (Forrer et al. 2010). Therefore, PPPs are contract models intended to manage public services, as an alternative to a direct in-house management (direct management by public authorities or though state-own enterprises—SoEs). However, this is not equivalent to the privatization of public services, even when the partnership is executed through a long-term contract. This is because, in a PPP, CAs set the characteristics and scope of the infrastructure and services, and retain the ultimate responsibility for the quality and appropriateness thereof, together with the possibility to terminate the contract, eventually, if EOs prove unable to achieve the public goals set or to meet the required standards. Conversely, in privatized contexts, public authorities play a regulatory role, that is, setting a framework for the free deployment of competition among EOs, as the latter become the ultimate owners of infrastructure, or compete freely in a liberalized market for the delivery of services.

Figure 1.3 shows a synthesis of these three main approaches for the delivery of public interest services.

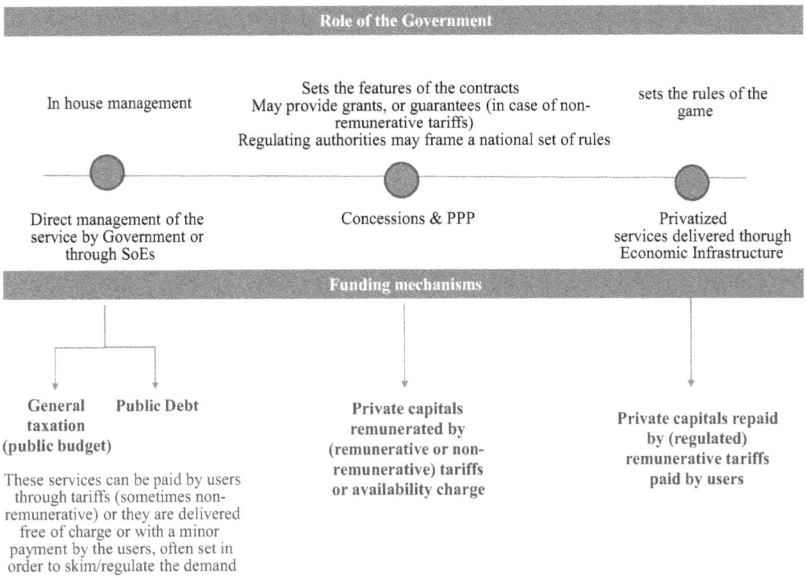

Fig. 1.3 Models for the delivery of public interest services. Source: Authors

1.3 Policy Goals Beyond PPP and the Challenges to Achieve Them

PPPs have become popular with the rise of New Public Management policies in the Anglo-Saxon countries as a means to increase public services efficiency and performance (a concept known as "value for money") and to reduce red tape, by lifting some of the constraints for the public sector and easing public bureaucracy. PPP projects can deliver "value for money" when they achieve the same outcomes at a lower cost (efficiency), and/or higher/better quality for services and innovative solutions at the same cost (added value), if compared to standard projects. Therefore, value for money in PPPs is mainly linked to the delivery of works and related services "on-time, on-budget and on-quality," through the whole life-cycle optimization of projects, which is achieved, inter alia, thanks to the efficient management of the required means and resources and the bundled nature of PPP contracts. More recently, public value literature considers PPPs as a way to foster collaborative co-production, capable of providing more innovative responses and improving services quality.

The global spread of PPPs is mainly rooted in macroeconomic reasons. PPPs have been widely used as an alternative to privatization policies, often opposed by public opinion, therefore, politically embarrassing.

PPPs' popularity is associated with the opportunity that it affords CAs to account investment "off balance sheet": in other words, the possibility of obtaining assets requiring substantial investments without increasing public debt. PPP contracts can also act as a filter, especially for user-fee-based projects, by skimming unfeasible and un-bankable projects. This is particularly true for projects only partially funded or guaranteed by the public sector. In these instances, the matching fund mechanism can mitigate the potential risk of misallocation of public money by excluding unrealistic projects.

Current research is often critical of the value for money and affordability of PPPs, and this is in spite of the widespread belief of many international institutions that these kinds of arrangements lead to more efficient and more effective outcomes for policy development. Indeed, there is a wide international consensus on the fact that PPPs, in many cases, facilitate the delivery of new infrastructure on time and on budget. Because of the difficulties in designing correct allocation of risks during the management phase or in incorporating innovative delivery solutions, in many cases PPP has not lived up to expectations.

Scholars are often critical of the capacity of the public and private sectors to develop mutual trust, which is needed to implement a long-term contract. Actually, the institutional and value-related differences between public and private players determine an over-formalization of the relationship through contractual obligations that could prove hardly enforceable, due to the information asymmetry between public and private subjects. Further, the variety of possible events that may occur during the contract life are often difficult to forecast and incorporate into contractual provisions. This issue can be particularly critical in contexts with weak institutions. Since PPPs are long-term contracts, it is indeed crucial to find the right balance between completeness and flexibility.

Despite the fact that contractual PPP is not a new concept, high barriers still exist which prevent its diffusion and consolidation: PPP has been applied to many sectors across the world with mixed results that, at times, have generated reluctance among policy makers and public managers.

The inherent contract complexity, the level of uncertainty typical of long-term transactions, and the oligopolistic features of the market are some of the issues making value for money difficult to achieve, especially when risk allocation is influenced by the need to attract private capitals (the issue is discussed in Chap. 2). Some relevant contracts across the globe experienced several implementation criticalities due to the need to renegotiate the contract, the failure of the SPV, or excess costs for users or the CA, just to quote a few. This has fueled arguments about the appropriateness of the contract type/policy. In fact, Teisman and Klijn (2002)) described PPPs as the "right proposal at the wrong time." The increased commitment of market players to public value, as discussed in Sect. 1.1, could be useful to overcome the drawbacks experienced so far and to stimulate the co-evolution of the public and private parties.

More recently, a growing body of literature has been discussing the importance of a stable institutional framework and a strong policy commitment for supporting the efficient and effective application of PPPs (Hodge and Greve 2017; Verhoest et al. 2014). Three main factors appear to be crucial for the development of PPPs: i) clear policies and political commitment; ii) appropriate legal and regulatory frameworks; and iii) dedicated PPP-supporting units. Explicit policies and long-term political commitment are crucial for creating legitimacy for PPP and for transforming it from an extraordinary approach into a standard option for the public sector, especially when developing complex investments or incorporating innovative solutions in the services delivery. An appropriate PPP legal and regulatory framework, including specific PPP laws, helps procuring authorities and market players to reduce uncertainty and transaction costs, thus fostering collaboration and transparency. PPP-supporting units may be crucial as competence hubs to support CAs and EOs, and to enhance the application of PPP, on a constant basis, through the collection and dissemination of good practices. However, the above-mentioned factors are not enough without an adequate set of competencies within CAs directly involved in transactions.

It is, therefore, essential, both at central and local levels, to build up strong competencies to structure, manage, monitor, and enforce PPP contracts. As discussed in Chap. 2, it is fundamental that public authorities have access to the most sophisticated skills to design the most appropriate PPP contract, based on the goals to attain and the relevant context, and to choose the right balance of risks/rewards to achieve value for money, innovation, and value added.

1.4 From Traditional to Strategic Procurement: Lessons from Covid-19 to Create a Shared Culture to Foster Partnership Between Public and Private Sectors

The extraordinary Covid-19 outbreak, faced by governments all around the world, sheds light on the importance of improving public procurement. This shall not be limited to the field of healthcare. An enhanced focus on the strategic role of procurement coupled with the value of public-private partnerships are twin goals that can be prioritized whenever the CAs act as sophisticated buyers (Vecchi et al. 2020).

More often than not, within the public sector, procurement has been perceived as a clerical function, mainly focusing on transparency and accountability (Table 1.1 shows the main differences between the two approaches). This culture hindered the development of inter-organizational relationships and trust: efforts to prevent corruption in public contracting, although justified, have generated a bureaucratic approach to procurement that stifles any attempt at contracting innovation and, more in general, many solutions that could better meet societal needs, including risk mitigation.

To overcome the limits of traditional public procurement, the public sector has relied on public-private collaborations, although, with mixed and not always fully appreciated results. Partnerships can prove crucial, also in crises like Covid-19, because they improve the flexibility of the public sector and its capacity to provide immediate answers to communities.

Table 1.1 Differences between conventional and strategic procurement

Conventional procurement	*Strategic procurement*
• Lowest bid selection criteria • Prioritizing cost savings • Transactional contractor relationships • Fragmented acquisition for narrowly defined products • Minimal attention to contractor business practices • Acquiring products for short-term needs	• Best value selection criteria • Prioritizing innovation • Partnership-based contractor relationship • Coordinated acquisition for integrated solutions • Strong understanding of contractor business processes (supply chain, risk management, ESG policies) • Acquiring products for long-term, risk-managed needs

Source: Vecchi et al. 2020

Disaster situations call for the immediate creation of reactive short-term collaborative relationships, also known as hastily generated partnerships (Busch and Givens 2013), between public and private entities. Such partnerships are not only fundamental to ensure resilience but, also, may pave the way to build up relationships of trust on a larger scale. Indeed, the development of relationships and trust allow collaborative procurement arrangements to function more effectively in complex policy areas by providing an opportunity for interested stakeholders to work closely together to address community problems.

Based on the lessons of global scale crises, such as Covid-19 pandemic, policy makers should consider areas of procurement that would have been less affected, had previous partnerships existed with EOs, by comparing the flexibility, rapidity, and business continuity that would have been offered by contractual agreements based on different levels of collaboration. Resilience-oriented procurement strategies, therefore, shall be based on the selection of reliable providers; the creation of a portfolio of providers to be called upon in case of emergency; and the use of contracts to allow flexibility and outcome-assurance (Bovaird and Quirk 2016).

In order to do this, co-designed solutions are needed, which, in turn, is possible only if the public sector is open and ready to negotiate with EOs, thus moving procurement from a compliance-based perspective to a risk-management and collaborative perspective. A strategic approach to procurement would also enable business resilience and innovation and implement other strategic public policies, as an economic stimulus for market organizations, for employment and, ultimately, as a driver of domestic growth.

The post Covid-19 period will certainly leave more room for the adoption of new practices in public procurement and PPP.

To make the most of strategic management of public procurement and PPP, however, it is fundamental to invest in the managerial competencies of the public sector, whose weaknesses are deemed to have been one of the main reasons behind the unmet promises of the previous public-private partnership season (Bloomfield 2006). Equally, the private sector should invest more in building up an adequate set of skills and competencies, with a view to providing solutions able to meet profit and public value goals at the same time. A shareable background of competencies and skills is crucial to create a common playing field to develop trust and, therefore, to co-create more sustainable, balanced, and innovative partnerships.

In conclusion, to allow and sustain a renewed approach to PPP, based on more balanced and sustainable contracts—that is where achieving public value becomes the main goal—it is fundamental that both public and private actors evolve. On one hand, public procurement should play a more strategic role; on the other hand, PPP should be chosen by EOs as a means to pursue their sustainability/purpose-driven corporate strategies, as discussed above in Sect. 1.1.

Bibliography

Baron, D. P. (2001). Private Politics, Corporate Social Responsibility, and Integrated Strategy. *Journal of Economics & Management Strategy, 10*(1), 7–45.

Bhattacharyya, S. S. (2010). Exploring the Concept of Strategic Corporate Social Responsibility for an Integrated Perspective. *European Business Review, 22*(1), 82–101.

Bloomfield, P. (2006). The Challenging Business of Long-Term Public-Private Partnerships: Reflections on Local Experience. *Public Administration Review, 66*(3), 400–411. http://www.jstor.org/stable/3843920.

Bovaird, T., & Quirk, B. (2016). Moving from Risk Avoidance to Assuring Public Policy Outcomes. *The Routledge Handbook of Global Public Policy and Administration, 258*, 1.

Busch, N., & Givens, A. (2013). Achieving Resilience in Disaster Management: The Role of Public-Private Partnerships. *Journal of Strategic Security, 6*(2), 1–19. https://doi.org/10.5038/1944-0472.6.2.1.

Carroll, A. B. (1979). A Three-Dimensional Conceptual Model of Corporate Performance. *The Academy of Management Review, 4*(4), 497. https://doi.org/10.2307/257850.

Carroll, A. B. (1991). The Pyramid of Corporate Social Responsibility: Toward the Moral Management of Organizational Stakeholders. *Business Horizons, 1*, 39–48.

Forrer, J., Kee, J. E., Newcomer, K. E., & Boyer, E. (2010). Public-private Partnerships and the Public Accountability Question. *Public Administration Review, 70*(3), 475–484. https://doi.org/10.1111/j.1540-6210.2010.02161.x.

Freeman, R. E., Harrison, J. S., Wicks, A. C., Parmar, B. L., & De Colle, S. (2010). *Stakeholder Theory: The State of the Art*. Cambridge: Cambridge University Press.

Garriga, E., & Melé, D. (2004). Corporate Social Responsibility Theories : Mapping the Territory. *Journal, 53*, 51–71.

Hartley, J., Sørensen, E., & Torfing, J. (2013). Collaborative Innovation: A Viable Alternative to Market Competition. *Public Administration Review, 73*(6), 821–830. https://doi.org/10.1111/puar.12136.

Hodge, G. A., & Greve, C. (2017). On Public–Private Partnership Performance: A Contemporary Review. *Public Works Management and Policy, 22*(1), 55–78. https://doi.org/10.1177/1087724X16657830.

Jensen, M. C. (2010). Value Maximization, Stakeholder Theory, and the Corporate Objective Function. *Journal of Applied Corporate Finance, 22*(1), 32–42.

McElhaney, K. (2009). A Strategic Approach to Corporate Social Responsibility. *Leader to Leader, 52*(1), 30–36.

Porter, M. E., & Kramer, M. R. (2006). Strategy and Society: The Link Between Competitive Advantage and Corporate Social Responsibility. *Harvard Business Review, December*, 78–93.

Porter, M. E., & Kramer, M. R. (2011). Creating Shared Value. *Harvard Business Review, February*, 62–77.

Teisman, G. R., & Klijn, E.-H. (2002). Partnership Arrangements: Governmental Rhetoric or Governance Scheme? *Public Administration Review, 62*(2), 197–205. https://doi.org/10.1111/0033-3352.00170.

Vecchi, V., Cusumano, N., & Boyer, E. J. (2020). Medical Supply Acquisition in Italy and the United States in the Era of COVID-19: The Case for Strategic Procurement and Public–Private Partnerships. *American Review of Public Administration*. https://doi.org/10.1177/0275074020942061.

Verhoest, K., Petersen, O. H., Scherrer, W., & Murwantara Soecipto, R. (2014). *Policy Commitment, Legal and Regulatory Framework, and Institutional Support for PPP in International Comparison: Indexing Countries' Readiness for Taking Up PPP*. Salzburg: University of Salzburg.

CHAPTER 2

Private Investments for Infrastructure

Veronica Vecchi, Francesca Casalini, and Niccolò Cusumano

Abstract The role of financial investors in infrastructure financing is key to closing the infrastructure gap and to sustaining growth since public budgets do not allow sufficient financing. This chapter reviews existing instruments for private infrastructure financing and discusses the policies that can be put in place to attract private investors. These policies include blended finance mechanisms that are intended to crowd-in money at industry/regional level, as well as more specific measures that sustain the attraction of capital at project level.

Keywords Infrastructure financing • Policies to attract investors • Project financing • Project bonds • Moral hazard

2.1 Investing in Infrastructure

Both PPP projects and privatized infrastructures are financed through a mix of debt and equity. As described in Chap. 1, equity can be invested in the project by corporate/industrial investors (listed or not listed), whose core business is the management of PPP/concession contracts, or by financial investors, such as infrastructure funds (listed or unlisted):

V. Vecchi et al., *Public Private Partnerships*,
https://doi.org/10.1007/978-3-030-65435-1_2

- Corporate industrial investors can invest directly by entering themselves into the contract with the contracting authority (CA), without setting up an SPV. Otherwise, they invest indirectly, by setting up an SPV. Their capital is fundamental during the investment stage, when the risk is higher; thanks to their industrial know-how they can manage and mitigate such risks.
- Financial investors generally invest equity in SPVs, especially during the management phase or in brownfield projects, where risks are limited or more predictable; otherwise, they invest in the equity of corporate/industrial players, especially into listed ones.

On the debt side, fundamentally, there are two approaches: either corporate financing or project financing. In corporate financing schemes, debt is raised directly by the industrial/corporate player, and the set-up of an SPV is not usually needed; in project-financing schemes, the SPV itself borrows capitals through a syndicated loan granted by a pool of banks or from bondholders when the SPV issues project bonds. The SPV is indeed a requirement in the case of a project-financing debt structure because it ring-fences the cash flow generated by the project, which, in principle, is the main form of guarantee provided (Gatti 2013), thus ensuring the provision of debt on a no- or limited-recourse basis. The assets of the SPV become collateral for the loans although they play a secondary role compared to project cash flows. This is in contrast to corporate finance where lenders rely on the borrower's creditworthiness for their loans. Furthermore, rights and obligations associated with an investment project are related to the SPV only.

For the reasons above, project financing is usually a much higher leveraged transaction compared to corporate financing. In a typical PPP project, up to 70%–80% of financing is procured in the form of senior debt while the share of equity does not normally exceed 20%–30%.

A higher financial leverage allows for optimization of the cost of the overall financial structure (Table 2.1).

One of the main challenges in infrastructure financing is attracting financial investors, such as infrastructure funds and pension funds. Their role is key to closing the infrastructure gap and to sustaining growth since public budgets do not allow sufficient financing, even more so after the Covid-19 pandemic. Conversely, global financial assets are

Table 2.1 Main differences between corporate financing and project financing

	Corporate financing	*Project financing*
Guarantees for financing	Assets of the borrower	Project assets
Effect on financial elasticity	Reduction of financial elasticity for the borrower	No or heavily reduced effect for sponsors
Accounting treatment	On-balance sheet	Off-balance sheet (the only effect will be either disbursement to subscribe equity in the SPV or for subordinated loans)
Main variables underlying the granting of financing	Solidity of balance sheet Profitability	Future cash flows
Degree of leverage utilizable	Depends on effects on borrower's balance sheet	Depends on cash flow generated by the project (leverage is usually much higher)

Source: Gatti (2014)

sufficient to meet the infrastructure financing needs, but the challenge is how to channel them, by enhancing the risk-return profiles of new and sometimes vulnerable investments and generating sustained impact on the ground.

Private capital can be more easily attracted to infrastructure operated in a competitive environment or for privatized infrastructure, such as markets that are dominated by private players, often listed and, therefore, able to raise funds from capital markets. In PPP/concession contracts, where private players are selected to build/revamp infrastructure and operate the service, financing is more critical. This is particularly true for bond financing, which represents a small fraction (about 10%) of the overall debt financing (Gatti et al. 2019) (Box 2.1).

2.2 Blended Finance: A Meso-Level Partnership to Attract Investors (also) in Infrastructure

As explained in Chap. 1, blended finance (BF) is a form of meso-level cooperation used to crowd-in private capitals in riskier investments, such as infrastructure PPPs, especially in emerging countries. This form of finance is also used to attract investors in impact investing and SMEs financing. BF is a "structuring approach" rather than an investment approach; it means

Box 2.1 How to combine loans and bonds to improve private capital attraction

In order to ensure a sufficient amount of private capitals to contribute to the closure of infrastructure gap, in the framework of new banking rules (Basel III rules), there is the need for capital market instruments, such as project bonds, to complement bank funding. In addition, securitization of bank loans could support lending, broaden the investors' base, and diversify risks, while also developing capital market instruments (Gatti 2014).

However, considering their long-term expertise in infrastructure financing, banks will continue to play a significant role as lenders during the construction phase of an infrastructure project finance transaction. Indeed, institutional investors are less familiar with the complexities of infrastructure projects and the risks assessment. Instead, they are more interested in the opportunity to invest in assets with a stable cash flow. Therefore, the role of the latter could be to step in during the operational phase by refinancing existing bank loans with a project bond issue.

Bank loans have several advantages vis-à-vis bonds to finance the construction phase:

1. Banks provide a fundamental monitoring role as watchdog.
2. Infrastructure projects need a gradual disbursement of funds (the drawdown of debt is consistent with the implementation of works during the investment phase) and sometimes debt restructuring is needed to cope with project changes that may occur; bank lending offers such required flexibility.

Once the project moves into the operation phase and project risks are lower, loans can be refinanced with other capital market instruments, such as project bonds. This also allows banks to recycle capital to be invested in other greenfield projects.

that it is meant to structure together layers of money coming from different investors, with different profiles, mandates, and expectations. Such structuring approach is based on mixing public and private capital in a common and complementary investment scheme where public or philanthropic sources are used as a catalyst to increase private sector investments and sustainable development, mostly in developing countries.

BF mechanisms involve the following actors:

- public investors, both those with a development mandate and those with a commercial and development mandate—such as various multilateral development banks (MDBs);
- private investors;
- philanthropic investors (such as foundations).

A BF approach is based on three principles: Leverage, Impact, and Return.

- Leverage: meaning using scarce development finance and philanthropic funds to attract private capital through de-risking mechanisms.
- Impact: BF is aimed at generating financial additionality to fund investments able to drive social, environmental, and economic progress; blending mechanisms also allow for the mixing of public and private skills to increase the effectiveness of development-related investments.
- Returns: investments have different returns, ranging from concessional (see below) to market rate, depending on the type of investors involved; the goal of BF mechanisms is to generate returns for private investors in line with market expectations based on the level of perceived risk.

BF mechanisms are intended to support bankable or quasi-bankable projects. For bankable projects, those that meet the expectations of lenders, BF is meant to increase available funding (the so-called financial additionality) or to provide technical assistance for maximizing the impact as well as reducing political/regulatory risks. For quasi-bankable projects, those that are potentially interesting for lenders, BF allows risk mitigation to attract private capital. Non-bankable projects are not the focus of blended finance since the probability of failure and financial loss is much too high (Convergence 2020).

The most used blended finance models are the following:

1. Co-investment of concessional capital and private capital is the most used type. Public or philanthropic investors provide funds on below-market terms (also known as, on a concessional basis) within a capital structure in order to lower the overall cost of capital, thus making the project viable, or to provide an additional layer of protection to private investors, thus attracting them. Concessional capital includes first-loss debt or equity, investment-stage grants, and debt or equity that bears risk at below-market financial returns, to mobilize private sector investment. The use of concessional capital allows for the financing to be structured with different layers of risk, through:

    - A-shares and senior notes to attract institutional investors;
    - B-shares, such as mezzanine capital to attract private investors with an appetite for risk;
    - Junior tranches of debt and first-loss equity shares dedicated to development finance investors (MDBs, donors, or impact investors).

    The capital structure can also include a grant. The combination of grant, guarantee (which is a second form of BF structure), and concessional debt or equity provide greater protection to traditional investors who provide common equity and senior debt.

2. Guarantee and insurance. Public or philanthropic investors provide credit enhancement through guarantees or insurance on below-market terms.
3. Technical assistance facilities. The transaction is associated with grant-funded technical assistance that can be used before or after completion of the investment, to strengthen its commercial viability and impact.
4. Design/Preparation funds that provide grants to support the design or preparation of the transaction.

Blending money can happen at fund or project level. In most cases, the preferred option is to blend financing at fund level in order to generate a higher leverage effect in terms of increased attraction of private capital.

Funds are pools of private or public-private capital, where blending occurs at the capital structure level for public-private funds or at project level (Convergence 2020). Public development resources (sometimes including support from philanthropic investors) come in the majority of cases from facilities, which are earmarked allocations of money; these resources can be invested in development projects through a range of instruments, including the purchasing of shares in collective vehicles such as funds. There is no blending of money in facilities; instead, facilities provide finance to blend money further down at the fund or project level.

2.3 Specific Policy Measures to Attract Investors in PPP Transactions

If BF mechanisms are intended to crowd-in money at industry/regional level, especially for the achievement of development goals, many governments and some supra-national institutions, such as MDBs, also in mature economies, have introduced specific measures to respond to and counterbalance the shortage of capital for infrastructure development, especially targeted to PPP projects. Such measures may be based on five different mechanisms (Gatti et al. 2019; Hellowell et al. 2014; Vecchi et al. 2017), namely:

1. grants, to reduce the capital requirements of the project or to integrate revenues;
2. availability-based payments, to neutralize the demand risk while leaving the performance risk with the private investor;
3. credit-enhancement, such as the very common “minimum payment guarantee,” to reduce or eliminate the credit default risk for lenders, that is, either banks or (more specifically) project bondholders;
4. direct provision of debt and equity capital by government, public financial agencies, or development banks, to offset the liquidity gap;
5. other measures, among them, favorable taxation.

These facilities are not an alternative to blended finance mechanisms since they offer support to specific projects and, therefore, can be combined with blended mechanisms to sustain a stable capital attraction. Table 2.2 provides details of these five main measures.

Table 2.2 Main policy instruments to support capital attraction in PPP projects

Policy measures	*Features*	*Effects*
1. Grant	1. Lump sum capital grant	Reducing the need for private capital
	2. Revenue grant: 2.1 Periodic fixed amount (mitigating the demand risk) 2.2 Revenue integration (it leaves the demand risk on the private player)	Increasing the revenue volume and stability, when the economic operator (EO) retains the demand risk and tariffs are set at socially acceptable levels. It may generate moral hazard, by reducing the incentive for a performing operation
	3. Grant on debt interests	Reducing the amount of interests due to the debt provider. Rarely used
2. Availability payment	1. Availability payment is typical in the social infrastructure sector, where the main user is the public sector. In some cases, availability payment can be used also for economic infrastructure, in which case the service can be delivered free of charge to users or tariffs are collected by the public authority	Eliminating the demand risk Generally, the EO bears the performance risk. It is recommended especially for economic infrastructure instead of the minimum revenue payment
3. Guarantee on debt	1. Minimum revenue guarantee	The demand risk is partially retained by CAs, committed to guaranteeing a certain level of revenues, generally those necessary to ensure the debt service at a pre-set level of DSCR (debt service cover ratio)
	2. Guarantee in case of default	The guarantee covers the payment of outstanding debt (both principal and interest) in the case of private player's default
	3. Guarantee in case of refinancing	In the context of "mini perm" financial structure (i.e. a debt structure that can—soft mini perm—or must—hard mini perm—be refinanced after the construction phase), the guarantee repays lenders if the private player fails to refinance the loan at maturity, especially in the event of increased interest rates or changed market liquidity

(*continued*)

Table 2.2 (continued)

Policy measures	*Features*	*Effects*
4. Provision of capital	1. Subordinated (junior) debt	Enhancing the credit quality of the senior debt
	2. Debt: 2.1 Pari passu condition 2.2 At lower interest rate	Providing debt capital at competitive market condition In some circumstances, it can be provided also at lower rates, thus helping the project to meet the expectation of other debt capital investors, in terms of interest rate, DSCR, and maturity
	3. Equity: 3.1 At market conditions 3.2 At more advantageous conditions	Providing equity to fill the equity gap; to reduce the financial leverage, and, therefore, the exposure to credit risk; to offer downside protection or upside leverage to private equity holders
	1. Favorable taxation: 1.1 Favorable taxation schemes for SPV 1.2 Favorable taxation schemes for equity investors	Introducing lower corporate taxation to sustain the general viability of the project (the effect is to increase free cash flow to operation); or lower taxation on "qualified dividends" and long-term capital gains

Source: Authors

The role of MDBs proves fundamental to facilitate access to private capitals and financial markets, for example, to bond financing, especially in emerging markets, where regulatory, construction, and demand risks can be significantly high. However, facilities to attract investors must be designed to prevent situations of moral hazard. Any form of guarantee that limits the construction risks can seriously reduce the incentives to deliver the infrastructure on time and on budget and, at the same time, generate public debt. In this context, the role of MDBs can be fundamental to crafting balanced facilities and to supporting governments in developing a feasible projects' pipeline and strengthening the applicable legal framework. As regards the need for mitigation of the demand risk, the use of availability charge payments could be a useful solution, as experienced in Europe after the financial crisis (Vecchi et al. 2015). Availability charge could represent the dominant payment mechanism of the PPP transaction.

Alternatively, the competent authority could use it during the ramp-up period according to a statistical approach based on previous tolls paid by users, keeping the option to switch it to regular toll-based payment, cashed in by the concessionaire when the demand becomes more stable and mature.

However, when a project is heavily supported by public funds or guarantees, economic operators (EOs) may have no incentive to:

1. form optimal bidding consortia;
2. undertake careful and reliable assessments of the project's features (e.g. capital, operational costs, and demand); or
3. select the best contractors and ensure the project's overall efficiency.

In other words, public guarantees can undermine the EOs' incentives to identify, monitor, and minimize project risks and thereby generate substantial additional fiscal burdens for governments and taxpayers (Box 2.2).

Box 2.2 Strategic behavior in PPP contracts protected by guarantees and the role of public sector skills

PPP contracts should be able to mitigate the principal-agent problems typically associated with traditional procurement, such as conflicting goals, information asymmetries, and diverging levels of risk aversion. PPP does so by transferring many project risks to private parties, thereby providing stronger incentives for the latter to perform accordingly. However, if incentives are weak, PPPs become similar to standard procurement contracts. In PPP, and in the public-procurement literature in general, evidence has been produced in relation to (1) comprehensive and rigorous contracts, (2) measurable output indicators, and (3) credible sanctions to manage the principal-agent relation (which is the basis of PPP transactions) and to prevent moral hazard by strengthening incentives to deliver high-quality services. These measures are generally suitable for transferring endogenous risks to the concessionaire, such as those related to design, construction, operation, and maintenance, thereby avoiding or reducing the risk of renegotiation. Contract renegotiation, which is defined as a change in the original contractual terms and

(*continued*)

Box 2.2 (continued)

conditions (as opposed to an adjustment that takes place within a contract's provisions), is one of the most pervasive problems in PPP because the underpinning contracts tend to be incomplete. Renegotiations of PPP contracts also result from imperfections in the judicial and regulatory system, economic shocks, and weaknesses in the institutional environment. The most problematic issues arises when a public authority retains the demand risk (partially or totally, directly or indirectly), which is an exogenous risk, as a consequence of revenue guarantees to make projects more bankable and appealing for institutional investors: in these cases, EOs have stronger incentives to adopt strategic behaviors. Strategic bidders are those who include technical or financial features in their bids, which they may not be fully able to meet, with the sole purpose of winning the contract. Such bidders assume the CAs will activate the guarantee and, ultimately, renegotiate or review the contract to ensure its success. In fact, public guarantees exacerbate the problem of adverse selection, which is quite common in the general public-procurement system, where the preferred bidder may be the most optimistic bidder rather than the best one (a situation known as "winner's curse"). This situation arises from strategies of "low balling" and from optimistic bias in traffic, revenue, or cost forecasts. To overcome these problems public sector competence in PPP transactions proves fundamental to counterbalance the aggressive behaviors of the private sector. To understand the role of public sector skills, we can refer to the results obtained by an agent-based simulation model (Vecchi et al. 2016), based on 120,000 simulations. Figure 2.1 presents a plot of the results; it considers the probability of awarding the project to a strategic bidder (vertical axis) as a function of the environmental propensity for strategic behavior (horizontal axis) for different skill levels of the awarding authority (unskilled; skilled; highly skilled).

The simulation is not relevant for the reported figures on their own, which are the consequence of the specific values of each real scenario included in the simulation. Rather, it shows a robust trend highlighting the fact that the probability of awarding the contract to a strategic bidder falls as the skills of the authority increase, especially

(*continued*)

Box 2.2 (continued)

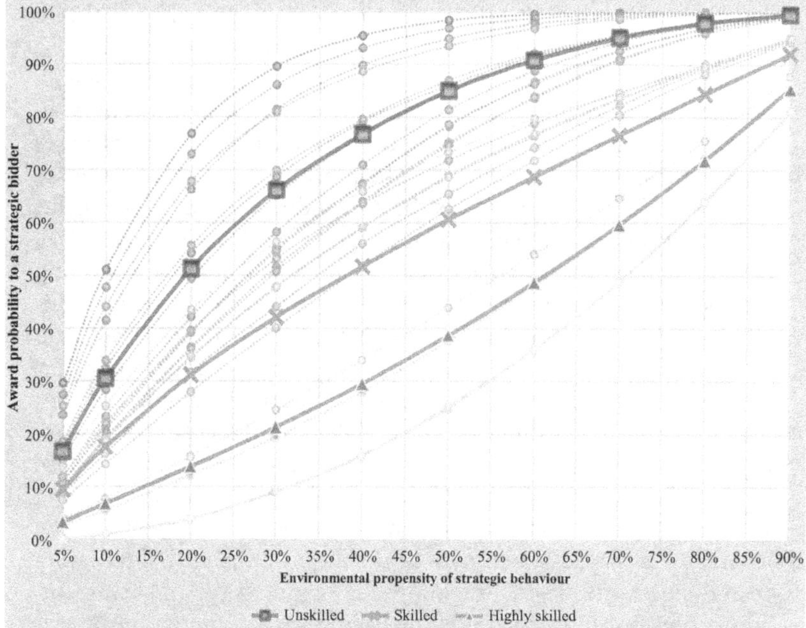

Fig. 2.1 The role of skills to reduce strategic bidding (Source: Vecchi et al. 2016)

in contexts with a high propensity to strategic bidding, such as those with weaker institutions or high corruption.

As discussed above, when certain kinds of guarantees are offered in PPP contracts to attract private capitals (e.g., a minimum revenue guarantee, a credit guarantee, or an availability charge), the likelihood of strategic behavior among market participants and the risk of adverse selection may increase. Therefore, it is fundamental, as shown by the simulation, to involve skilled public managers or consultants in the design and implementation of a PPP awarding procedure to reduce information asymmetries or the risk of selecting a strategic contractor, who may rely on the guarantee in order to compensate for poor performance. The same is true also in contexts where there is a higher probability of strategic behaviors.

References

Convergence. (2020). *How to Mobilize Private Investment At Scale in Blended Finance.*

Gatti, S. (2013). *Project Finance in Theory and Practice: Designing, Structuring, and Financing Private and Public Projects.* (Academic P). Elsevier.

Gatti, S. (2014). *Government and Market Based Instruments and Incentives to Stimulate Long-Term Investment Finance in Infrastructure.* OECD Working Paper.

Gatti, S., Casalini, F., Colla, P., & Vecchi, V. (2019). *An Empirical Analysis of Factors Responsible for the Use of Capital Market Instruments in Infrastructure Project Finance.* Working Paper Commissioned by the Asian Development Bank, Asia Infrastructure Insight.

Hellowell, M., Vecchi, V., & Caselli, S. (2014). Return of the State? An Appraisal of Policies to Enhance Access to Credit for Infrastructure-Based PPPs. *Public Money & Management.*

Vecchi, V., Casalini, F., & Gatti, S. (2015). Attracting Private Investors: The EU Project Bond Initiative and the Case of A11 Motorway BT – Public Private Partnerships for Infrastructure and Business Development: Principles, Practices, and Perspectives. In S. Caselli, G. Corbetta, & V. Vecchi (Eds.) (pp. 101–118). New York: Palgrave Macmillan US. https://doi.org/10.1057/9781137541482_6.

Vecchi, V., Amadio, S., Cusumano, N., Borgonovo, E., & Gatti, S. (2016). *Addressing Adverse Selection in PPP Tenders: A Micro-Economic Approach.* Research Paper.

Vecchi, V., Hellowell, M., & Casalini, F. (2017). Issues and Trends in Project Finance for Public Infrastructure BT – Structured Finance: Techniques, Products and Market. In S. Caselli & S. Gatti (Eds.) (pp. 127–152). Cham: Springer International Publishing. https://doi.org/10.1007/978-3-319-54124-2_6.

CHAPTER 3

PPP Legal Framework

Velia M. Leone

Abstract This chapter analyzes PPP under a legal perspective. Since there are several differences across jurisdictions in the legal treatment of PPP contracts, and there are no binding rules at international level, this chapter is focused on the European Union framework, which is one of the most advanced. It could provide a reference for emerging countries which are approaching PPP and are drafting national legislation on PPP contracts. The main focus of this chapter is on the development of legal provisions applying to PPPs, and, in particular, on the EU Concessions Directive and the fundamental concept of operating risk, i.e. the risk that has to be transferred on the private partner in concession contracts.

Keywords EU Court case law • EU Concession Directive • Operating risk • EPEC • Procedural aspects

3.1 The Development of an EU Legal Framework on PPP

This chapter examines PPPs from a legal standpoint. Since legal systems vary from one national context to the other, and considering there are no binding rules at international level, the natural choice was to focus on EU

V. Vecchi et al., *Public Private Partnerships*,
https://doi.org/10.1007/978-3-030-65435-1_3

legislation, which is both comprehensive and binding on a number of countries. That said, as seen in previous chapters, originally, the notion and practice of PPPs do not stem from legal provisions. Rather, they are the result of a complex phenomenon which developed as a practice over time in connection with the progressive scarcity of public funds. Also, more strategically, it developed as a trend to reduce the State's active role in the market, that is, from owner of infrastructure to service provider.

At international level, and especially in the financial and economic sectors, PPP contracts had been negotiated and signed long before entering the radar of lawmakers, at EU or national level. This is because PPP contracts are inherently a very flexible and multi-disciplinary response to the need for better infrastructure and services of higher quality. This ambitious result can be obtained through structured cooperation between public and private sectors, allowing the best results, beneficial to both parties, through a combination of different arrangements, with a distinctive financial purpose.

As PPPs increasingly spread across Europe, the EU institutions, especially the Commission, started to focus on them with a view to ensuring that such contracts complied with the EU rules on public contracts and concessions. The first time PPPs were analyzed with a more systematic EU law approach was in the Green Paper on public-private partnerships and Community law on public contracts and concessions, issued by the EU Commission in 2004 (the Green Paper).[1] The purpose of the Green Paper was to examine PPPs from the perspective of EU legislation and principles in order to provide a survey of the different types of contract and identify an appropriate framework for its encasing into the EU legal provisions on public procurement and concessions.

As expressly stated in the Green Paper, this approach was based on the assumption that "any act, whether it be contractual or unilateral, whereby a public entity entrusts the provision of an economic activity to a third party must be examined in the light of the rules and principles resulting from the Treaty, particularly as regards the principles of freedom of establishment and freedom to provide services [...], which encompass in particular the principles of transparency, equality of treatment, proportionality and mutual recognition."[2] The Green Paper describes PPP contracts as "forms of cooperation between public authorities and the world of

[1] Communication dated 30.4.2004 COM (2004) 327 final.

[2] Section 1.2, point 8 of the Green Paper.

business which aim to ensure the funding, construction, renovation, management or maintenance of an infrastructure or the provision of a service"[3] and provides first guidance on how they should be construed according to the EU legal framework on public contracts.

The Green Paper identifies the general characteristics of PPPs, as follows:

- relatively *long duration of the relationship*, involving cooperation between the public and the private partner on different aspects of a specific project;
- *method of funding the project*, involving a significant role played by the private sector, sometimes by means of complex arrangements including various players, with different expertise and competencies. Nonetheless, public funds—in some cases even rather substantial—may be added to the private funds;
- *important role of the economic operator* (EO), participating at different levels and stages in the project (design, completion, implementation, funding). Conversely, the public partner concentrates primarily on defining the objectives to be achieved in terms of public interest, quality of services provided, and pricing policy. The public sector takes responsibility for monitoring compliance with these objectives;
- appropriate *allocation of risks between the public and the private partner*, to whom the risks generally borne by the public sector are transferred. However, PPP contracts do not necessarily mean that the private partner assumes all the risks, or even the major share of the risks linked to a specific project. The precise distribution of all risks involved in a particular project is, finally, identified on a case-by-case basis, according to the respective ability of the concerned parties to assess, control, and cope with each individual risk.

Bearing in mind the above-mentioned features, the Green Paper draws a fundamental distinction between:

- PPPs of a *purely contractual nature*, that is, when the partnership between the public and the private sector is based solely on contractual links; and
- PPPs of an *institutional nature*, that is, involving cooperation between the public and the private sector within an ad hoc entity.

[3] Section 1.1, point 1 of the Green Paper.

Notwithstanding the different models used, throughout the EU and worldwide, the Green Paper concluded the scope of PPP contracts is aimed at the provision of services or works to contracting authorities (CAs), for a consideration, and, therefore, they qualify as "public contracts," according to the interpretation of EU Court of Justice (Court) (see Box 3.1).

Therefore, as PPPs are public contracts used by the CAs for the acquisition of services, including works, they involve the expenditure of public money. This specific nature of PPP contracts requires that the selection of the private partner falls within the realm of application of EU Internal Market rules and applicable principles, in particular, to public procurement and concessions. Moreover, they are encompassed by the public procurement directives,[4] which are "essentially aimed at protecting the interests of traders established in a Member State who wish to offer goods or services to contracting authorities established in another Member State and, to that end, to avoid both the risk of preference being given to national tenderers or applicants whenever a contract is awarded by the contracting authorities and the possibility that a body governed by public law may choose to be guided by considerations other than economic ones."[5]

In brief, according to the Green Paper, the rules applicable to the selection of the EOs are a consequence of the definition of the contractual relationship which that party enters into with CAs.

Having established the "public contract" nature of PPPs, then, it is important to assess whether this type of contract should be qualified as "public procurement" or "concession" contracts in order to determine their applicable rules. The Green Paper does not encase PPPs into a single specific contractual model, leaving such qualification open for a case-by-case analysis.

In this context, it should be stressed that, under EU law, the only two types of public contracts—that is, those aimed at the acquisition of works, goods, and services by CAs—are procurement and concession contracts. Therefore, all PPPs must fall within one of these two categories. The EU Directive on Concessions 2014/23/EU (Concessions Directive) clarifies

[4] It should be noted that when the Green Paper was issued, there was no specific directive on concessions. In those days, the public procurement directives provided a minimum set of rules on works concessions only.

[5] Green Paper, quoting the Court on Judgement in joint cases C-285/99 and C-286/99, Impresa Lombardini v. ANAS (November 27, 2001).

Box 3.1 The notion of public contract under EU rules

The Court held that the concept of *public works contracts* (or public service contracts) within the meaning of the public procurement directives requires that:

- the contractor undertakes to carry out the works/service—that is, the scope of the contract—for a *consideration* and the *obligations under the contract are legally binding, meaning that their execution must be legally enforceable*;
- these works or services are carried out *for the CA's immediate economic benefit*, so that they qualify as contract "for a pecuniary interest"[6] on both sides;
- the scope of public works or service contracts is the realization of works or services "corresponding to the requirements specified by the contracting authority." To verify if a CA has specified its requirements within the meaning of that provision, the CA must have taken measures to define the type of the work/service required or, at the very least, have had a decisive influence on its outline (Judgment of the Court, March 25, 2010, C-451/08, Helmut Müller GmbH).

The 2014 Directives enlist the notion of public contract, as developed by the Court. In particular, Directive 2014/24/EU on public contracts provides that:

- EU rules on public procurement "are not intended to cover all forms of disbursement of public funds, but only those aimed at the *acquisition* of works, supplies or services for consideration by means of a public contract. It should be clarified that such acquisitions of works, supplies or services should be subject to this Directive whether they are implemented through purchase, leasing, or other contractual forms" (recital 4, emphasis added);
- *"The notion of acquisition should be understood broadly in the sense of obtaining the benefits of the works, supplies or services in question, not necessarily requiring a transfer of ownership to the contracting authorities"* (recital 4, emphasis added);

[6] Such interest is to be identified in any form of economic consideration received by EOs, leaving aside the legal definitions.

(continued)

Box 3.1 (continued)

- "Procurement" is "the acquisition by means of a public contract of works, supplies or services by one or more contracting authorities from economic operators *chosen by those contracting authorities*, whether or not the works, supplies or services are intended for a public purpose" (Article 1, par. 2, emphasis added);
- "'public contracts' means contracts *for pecuniary interest* concluded in writing between one or more economic operators and one or more contracting authorities and having as their object the execution of works, the supply of products or the provision of services" (Article 2, par.1, no.5, emphasis added).

the fundamental distinction between public procurement and concession contracts: namely, the latter requires EOs to bear the so-called operating risk, connected to the exploitation of the works or service, encompassed in the contract scope.

Consequently, within PPPs having contractual nature, the Green Paper identifies two general models, namely:

- the "concession model," where there is a direct link between private operators and end-users. In other words, EOs provide services to the public, "in place of"—yet under the control of—the public partner. The remuneration consists of charges levied on the end-users of the services and, if necessary—for example, when they are not sufficient from a business perspective—supplemented by subsidies from public authorities.
- the so-called PFI model, whereby EOs carry out and operate infrastructure on behalf of the public authority and the remuneration is executed through regular payments by the CAs. These payments may be fixed or variable, on the basis, for example, of the availability of the works or their ancillary services, or even the level of use of the infrastructure.

That said, nowadays, the above-mentioned difference between these two models is no longer useful to distinguish between public procurement and concessions, as both types must encompass the proper allocation of operating risk to EOs in order to be considered PPP contracts. Such further developments were envisaged already in the Green Paper itself, which paved the way for them, when establishing that—irrespective of the contractual model chosen—the success of a PPP depends, to a large extent, on a "comprehensive contractual framework for the project, and on the optimum definition of the elements which will govern its implementation,"[7] such as:

- the "*appropriate assessment and optimum distribution of the risks* between the public and the private sectors, according to their respective ability to assume these risks"[8] (emphasis added);
- the "mechanisms to evaluate the performance"[9] of the EO.

Finally, the Green Paper stressed another important element, that is, the "economic and financial stability of a project,"[10] which implies:

- on the one hand, the duration of the PPP contracts must be set so that it does not limit open competition beyond what is required to ensure that the investment is paid off and there is a reasonable return for EOs; and
- on the other hand, PPP contracts must be able to evolve in line with changes in the macro-economic or technological environment, and with general interest requirements, as long as such possibility is provided for in compliance with the principles of equality of treatment and transparency. Thus, the awarding procedure documents may provide for automatic adjustment clauses or stipulate re-negotiation clauses. The latter must identify precisely the circumstances and conditions under which adjustments could be made to the contract, in a sufficiently clear way, so as to allow the EOs participating in the awarding procedure to interpret them unequivocally and submit their tenders accordingly.

In light of the essential elements of PPPs, as identified in the Green Paper and the following case law and legislation, it is to be concluded that, *nowadays, PPP contracts—in order to comply with the qualifying features*

[7] Section 2.3.1., point 45 of the Green Paper.
[8] Section 2.3.1., point 45 of the Green Paper.
[9] Section 2.3.1., point 45 of the Green Paper.
[10] Section 2.3.1., point 46 of the Green Paper.

that make them a useful and effective tool to achieve best results through cooperation between EOs and CAs—must be construed as a concession. Therefore, the following paragraphs concentrate on the identification and assessment of the operating risk since the distinctive character of concession contracts is a well-balanced and effective transfer of it to EOs.

3.2 Court Case Law on Concessions and the Concessions Directive: No More Ambiguities and False Myths

A pivotal role in fostering the evolution of EU law is played by the Court's case law in relation to the interpretation and evolution of primary and secondary legislation. This is because the Court not only interpreted and clarified, but also developed and even created principles applicable in the field of public procurement—to both public procurement contracts and concessions—often paving the way to further developments. This osmotic relationship gives rise to a virtual circle thanks to which the EU legislator has progressively included the Court's findings and guidelines in legislative reforms. If this is the case in all areas of EU legislation, it is even truer in the field of procurement and concessions. It is a field where the Court's law-generating function has led, for example, to the creation of different new legal arrangements—by case law and, only later, also legislation—such as, in house contracting, the possibility of using third parties' capacities, and so on. Additionally, it has led to the shaping of general principles which are to be considered immanent in the rules themselves and, therefore, must guide the parties—on the public and private side—both in the interpretation of the legislative provisions and in the conduct to be followed during awarding procedures and the execution of contracts, even in areas which were not specifically regulated by legal rules.

The evolution of EU regulation on concessions is no exception to this general backdrop.

Indeed, in terms of legal qualification, the Concessions Directive codified and clarified the principles and guidance on operating risk already laid down by the Court. Among other outcomes, these findings also overcame the distinction—in terms of applicable rules—between the awarding of works and service concessions. The concept of operating risk has been interpreted by the Court, on several occasions, progressing with the identification of its main features through subsequent refinements. The ultimate result of the case law of the Court is the possibility of using concession contracts, even in the context of highly regulated sectors, subject to null or just negligible market fluctuations. By so doing, the Court denied any relevance to the actual quantification of the operating risk.

Bearing in mind the pivotal role of the operating risk, for a contract to qualify as concession, the Court has specified:[11]

- it is necessary to establish whether the service provider takes the risk of operating the service. Even where, at the outset, that risk is very limited, by reason of the public law arrangements governing the organization of the service—that is, controlled prices—it is necessary CAs transfer to EOs all or at least a significant share of the risk;
- the operational risk must be understood as the risk of exposure to the vagaries of the market, which may, among others, consist in:

  - competition from other operators
  - supply of the services not matching the demand
  - end-users' inability to pay for the services provided
  - costs of operating the services not being met by revenue
  - liability for harm or damage resulting from an inadequacy of the service;

- risks such as those linked to inadequate management or errors of previous judgment by EOs are not decisive for the purposes of classification as a public service contract or a service concession, since those risks may incur in any type of contract, whether it be a public contract or a concession.

Conversely, the Court's case law has not yet reached a consistent and unambiguous position on the need for concessions to be based on a three-party relationship, that is, whereby concessionaires may only recoup their investments through tariffs paid by end-users. The Court went as far as stating that such three-party relationship represents *one form of remuneration* for concessions, without, however expanding on other possible types. This step forward by the Court may have paved the way to the evolution

[11] See, among others, Eurawasser, C-206/08, 10 September 2009; Privater Rettungsdienst, C-274/09, 10 March 2011; Norma-A SIA, C-348/10, 10 November 2011.

of the concept of availability risk. Concessions based on supply/availability risk only require two counterparts, namely CAs—representing the public interest and paying on behalf of the end-user or, in any case, without their direct involvement in the remuneration—and EOs. This point was clarified only with the publication of the Concessions Directive, which took good note of previous case law of the Court as, in recital 18, it identifies the essential features of a concession, as follows: "The main feature of a concession, the right to exploit the works or services, always implies the transfer to the concessionaire of an operating risk of economic nature involving the possibility that it will not recoup the investments made and the costs incurred in operating the works or services awarded under normal operating conditions *even if a part of the risk remains with the contracting authority or contracting entity*" (emphasis added).

Moreover, to clarify the concept of concession contracts, so as to allow its wider use, the Concessions Directive further elaborates on the concept of "operating risk" to dispel many "false myths" often associated with it.

3.2.1 *The First Myth: "Operating Risk Must be Quantified So As to Reach a Certain Minimum Amount"*

Article 5 of the Concessions Directive states that: "The award of a works or services concession shall involve the transfer to the concessionaire of an operating risk in exploiting those works or services encompassing demand or supply risk or both. The concessionaire shall be deemed to assume operating risk where, under normal operating conditions, it is not guaranteed to recoup the investments made or the costs incurred in operating the works or the services which are the subject-matter of the concession. The *part of the risk transferred to the concessionaire shall involve real exposure to the vagaries of the market*, such that *any potential estimated loss incurred by the concessionaire shall not be merely nominal or negligible*" (emphasis added).

Consequently, pursuant to the Concessions Directive, operating risk must:

- be excluded in all those cases where CAs relieve EOs of any potential loss by ensuring a guaranteed minimum income equal to or greater than the investments made and the costs incurred for the performance of the contract;
- not be reduced to the risk of incurring a purely nominal or negligible potential loss.

However, it should be noted that the above requirements do not extend to impose that the operating risk reaches a pre-determined minimum amount, or that it necessarily has to be very high. In other words: ***there is no minimum threshold for operating risk, provided it is not negligible.***

The Concessions Directive—following the same line of reasoning already developed by the Court in the above-mentioned case law[12]—specifies that the extent of the risk can be limited by the market structure itself, reiterating that (recital 19): "The fact that the risk is limited from the outset should not preclude the qualification of the contract as a concession. This can be the case for instance in sectors with regulated tariffs or where the operating risk is limited by means of contractual arrangements providing for partial compensation including compensation in the event of early termination of the concession for reasons attributable to the contracting authority or contracting entity or for reasons of force majeure," provided there are no "sector-specific regulation[s]" or contractual arrangements totally eliminating the concessionaire's risk "by providing for a guarantee to the concessionaire on breaking even on investments and costs incurred for operating the contract."

Bearing this in mind, it is still advisable, whenever possible, to quantify the economic impact of operational risk on EOs in the specific concession contract. This exercise must necessarily be related to the number of investments and costs whose recovery would be jeopardized should the expected risks occur. As methodologic guidance, Recital 20 of the Concessions Directive provides that "for the purpose of assessment of the operating risk the net present value of all the investment, costs and revenues of the concessionaire should be taken into account in a consistent and uniform manner."

To conclude, the assessment of the amount of operating risk taken on by the concessionaire is, in fact, useful for ensuring contract maintenance. This is because the transfer of an operating risk which is only apparent, or, conversely, of an excessive operating risk could, respectively, modify the nature of the contract (from the original concession to public procurement[13]) or undermine the economic sustainability of the concession itself overtime.

[12] See footnote no. 11.

[13] As regards such modification in the nature of the contract, initially qualified as concession, see Judgment of the Court of 13 November 2008—Commission v Italy, C-437/07.

3.2.2 The Second Myth: "Operating Risk may Only be Based on Demand"

The Concessions Directive departs from the traditional approach to concessions—focused on infrastructures and services of economic nature, meaning they can be exploited on the basis of actual demand from end-users—by providing a wider and clearer scope for the definition of operating risk. Recital 20 and Article 5 of the Concessions Directive make it clear that operating risk may be based on demand, supply risk, or both. Consequently, demand risk is to be understood as "the risk on actual demand for the works or services which are the object of the contract," while supply risk is "the risk on the provision of the works or services which are the object of the contract, in particular the risk that the provision of the services will not match demand."[14]. Both risks imply that "under normal operating conditions", the concessionaire is "not guaranteed to recoup the investments made or the costs incurred in operating the works or the services which are the subject-matter of the concession."

Therefore, the possibility of relying on the sole supply risk is expressly provided for in the Concessions Directive. It is worth stressing that, according to the Concessions Directive, the two types of risk are absolutely equivalent and do not necessarily have to be both present: one of the two being present is sufficient to qualify a specific contract as a concession. Moreover, it should be highlighted that—as interpreted by the Court in the above referred case law,[15] and further clarified by Recital 20 of the Concessions Directive—operating risk "should stem from factors which are outside the control of the parties. Risks such as those linked to bad management, contractual defaults by the economic operator or to instances of force majeure are not decisive for the purpose of classification as a concession, since those risks are inherent in every contract, whether it be a public procurement contract or a concession." This clarification is

[14] For infrastructure, supply risk can be declined as "availability risk"—according to Eurostat terminology—that is, the risk of guaranteeing continued functioning and use of the structures and the services connected to them, in order to meet, according to certain qualitative and quantitative standards, the needs—that is, the demand—of CAs, even when these needs change over time and involve higher costs for the concessionaire. The expression "availability risk", which initially appeared in the proposal for a directive on concessions submitted by the Commission—COM (2011) 897 final—was subsequently replaced by "supply risk" to give it a wider scope to concession contracts than just infrastructure.

[15] See footnote no. 11.

particularly relevant when concessions are based on supply/availability risk since, in such cases, operating risk could be confused with a simple risk of default (see par. 3.3). Therefore, this specific recital of the Concessions Directive provides the most enlightening evidence of the absolute equivalence of the two types of concession, namely those based on demand risk and those based on supply/availability risk.

3.2.3 *The Third Myth: "Concessions are Based on a Three-Party Relationship, Whereby the Concessionaire Recoups its Investments and Costs Through Tariffs (Actually or Virtually[16]) Paid by Users"*

The Concessions Directive finally clarifies residual ambiguities deriving from the Court's case law as regards the need for a "three-party relationship" in concession contracts.

Recital 18 of the Concessions Directive specifies that remuneration may not stem from payments by end-users since "it should be made clear that certain arrangements which are exclusively remunerated by a contracting authority or a contracting entity should qualify as concessions where the recoupment of the investments and costs incurred by the operator for executing the work or providing the service depends on the actual demand for or the supply of the service or asset."

In other words, operating risk consists in the lack of guarantees (for EOs) on the recovery of its investments and costs, regardless of the presence, or not, of a direct relationship with end-users. This is providing the risk of not recouping is related to events that, while being foreseeable and manageable by the concessionaire, are not directly attributable to it or its contractual performance, during the operational and management phase. As a result, the Concessions Directive expressly provides that, in addition to the "classic" types of concession contracts—where EOs are remunerated only or mainly by tariffs paid by end-users of the services and according to the (individual) demand for the service itself—the notion of concession also encompasses those contracts which are paid for—exclusively or mainly—by CAs, provided they entail an operating risk for the concessionaire.[17]

[16] For example, a virtual three-party relationship can be established when the so-called shadow tolls are paid to EOs, that is, when the concessionaire is remunerated through a fee based on individual use by end-users, but, in fact, the fee itself is paid by CAs.

[17] According to Eurostat's accounting rules, these concessions are defined PPP contracts (see par. 3.5).

These types of contracts—whereby EOs are paid by CAs—may include:

a. contracts where EOs are remunerated by CAs based on actual demand (although end-users do not directly pay tariffs to EOs)—for example, in the case of health services based on individual demand and paid accordingly;
b. contracts whose remuneration depends only on the supply of the work—that is, availability thereof—or the service, according to pre-defined qualitative and quantitative levels. This entails the risk of having to bear higher costs to guarantee the achievement of the aforementioned levels, such as, the efficient management and maintenance services of a non-economic infrastructure (school, prison, hospital) or certain equipment; as well as
c. contracts providing for both of the above mechanisms of payment.

3.3 The EPEC Guidance Note

Further clarification of the real scope of concessions, as defined by the Concessions Directive, was provided by the authoritative interpretation in the European PPP Expertise Centre's (EPEC) guidance note on "PPPs and Procurement Impact of the new EU Directives" of April 2016 (Guidance Note on Directives). The Guidance Note on Directives was meant to examine the possibilities afforded to CAs by the new directives, and, in particular, to verify their impact on the legal qualification and use of PPPs.

After summarizing the key issues arising from the new directives in those areas where they are expected to have a specific impact on PPPs, the Guidance Note on Directives focuses on the Concessions Directive by verifying whether PPPs may be included in the more sophisticated notion of concession as defined therein. The distinctive features of the Concessions Directive, in terms of procedural rules, may offer CAs more flexibility in the awarding of particular types of (often complex) contracts as PPPs. Moving from the above remark, the Guidance Note on Directives considers that while user-paid (demand-based) PPPs would almost always be concessions, most government-paid (availability-based) PPPs were not traditionally, or at least immediately, seen as concessions. However, the Concessions Directive, although not encompassing a legal definition of PPP, represents a remarkable break-through by fostering the notion of "supply risk" as a possible basis for operating risk. By so doing, it opens the possibility of procuring availability-based PPPs using the Concessions Directive. In any event, such qualification is conditional upon the actual transfer of operating risk—that is, economic risk foreseeable, but uncertain—to EOs.

In this context, the Guidance Note on Directives identifies key indicators useful for establishing whether:

- *the risk is transferred to EOs*. For instance, where a project benefits from guarantees from CAs, so as to make sure EOs are certain to at least break even on original investment costs, the risk is not transferred;
- *the risk may qualify as operating risk within the meaning of the Concessions Directive*. This is a specific type of risk, different than risks inherent in all public contracts. The following are examples of risks that cannot qualify as operating risk:
- force majeure—the transfer of a risk materializing from something that is *not foreseeable*, often identified as an *act of God*, is not sufficient to give rise to a concession, as other public contracts also have to deal with such risks;
- contractual default—that is, if a concessionaire bears the risk that it may default and consequently lose its investment, this is not sufficient to indicate that risk has been transferred, as this can happen in any public contract;
- bad management—that is, just because a concessionaire might not realize its expected profits because of its inefficient internal management, this does not mean that operating risk has been transferred, as public contracts also have to deal with these risks. However, it is not always easy to distinguish contracted-for risks from supply risks.

The above-mentioned issues are thoroughly analyzed in the Guidance Note on Directives, in particular, as regards supply/availability-based PPPs.

In these kinds of PPPs, EOs are not subject to the *vagaries of the market* as there is minimal competition for use, that is, demand is basically stable. However, even in these instances EOs are exposed to the vagaries of the market in relation to pricing of materials, supplies, and labor costs. Therefore, the key issue is to determine whether losses EOs might incur are due to the transfer of a supply risk rather than mismanagement.

According to the Guidance Note on Directives, in typical PPP, unlike conventional public contracts, significant risk transfer occurs because:

- the revenue stream does not match the cost liability being incurred. EOs, therefore, incur significant costs in building the asset in advance, but are not reimbursed or compensated for these costs until that asset is operating properly, together with the associated services;
- when EOs are faced with deductions through the payment mechanism (due to unavailability), they are expected to remedy the alleged defect from their own resources. This would reduce shareholders' returns and potentially involve making a call for contributions from equity participants.

Considering the above, the Guidance Note on Directives remarks that one of the main reasons for choosing a PPP structure is the contractual guarantee the asset will be carried out "on time" and "on budget,"[18] as well as in compliance with the expected quality standards. These guarantees are effective and efficient insofar as EOs are penalized financially—in a significant, not purely "cosmetic," or merely potential, way—if they fail to provide the initial asset and ancillary services, according to the agreed contractual terms. Consequently, the Guidance Note on Directives highlights the type of risks that—in PPP contracts based on supply/availability risk—EOs must assume and represent their operating risk, pursuant to the Concessions Directive. Furthermore, the impact of operating risk is different during the different execution phases of the PPP contract, namely:

- *in the initial phase of the contract*—EOs must design and deliver assets (which may consist of works or other fixed investments, for example machinery not easily removable) having a value which is retained throughout the contract duration and beyond. These assets are instrumental to the delivery of services by EOs. This is a fundamental transfer of supply risk. It requires EOs to make product and design choices at the outset, incurring the related investment costs. However, EOs' initial decisions and investments are rewarded only

[18] That is on the basis of the time schedule and predetermined costs.

through the stream of availability payments, achievable over the contract's complete and appropriate execution;[19]

- *during the operational phase of the contract*—Additional risks must be managed by EOs to ensure that assets, and associated services, remain in use and continue to function, in compliance with the agreed quality standards and the quantitative requirements set in the contract. These risks include many relief event risks (such as failure by a third-party utility provider or industry-wide industrial action and strikes), risk of failure of sub-contractors, some utility risks, insurance cost risks, maintenance costs, and so on. It is fundamentally important to manage these risks correctly for the proper functioning of the contract. If EOs are unable to do so—regardless of the circumstance of having, otherwise, fulfilled contractual obligations—they can be penalized through deductions from the availability payment, in addition to the classic contractual provisions relating to contractual breach, such as traditional penalties. Deductions are generally made by applying a predefined formula, progressively increasing the level of financial deductions as the duration of the sub-standard performance persists. In the worst-case scenario, persistent failure to perform according to the standards can lead EOs to forfeit the contract (through an event of default). In the event of unavailability of the asset and/or the service, CAs may step in to perform the services for a period of time while the issues leading to the service failures are addressed. Even in this hypothesis, the risk is transferred to EOs since the costs

[19] The fact that remuneration cannot take place before the assets involved in the investment come into operation does not prevent CAs—in order to ensure the initial balance of the contract—from providing an initial partial contribution—during the investment phase, and possibly also according to the progress of the works aimed at mitigating the debt exposure of EOs in the primary contractual phase. The aforementioned contribution does not constitute an availability payment—subject to operating risk—but a co-financing of the initial investment. Clearly, the value of this possible contribution must not be such as to eliminate construction risk for EOs and, therefore, in accordance with Eurostat rules, the same must be below 50% of the investment. Also it should be noted that the EPEC Guidance on statistical treatment of PPP of 2016 (the EPEC-PPP Guidance on Manual)—providing guidance on the interpretation of Eurostat's Manual on Government Deficit and Debt (implementation of ESA 2010)—clearly states that ways and timing of disbursement of the public contribution are considered *irrelevant with respect to the transfer of construction risk* (cf. Theme 2 and Theme 14.4 of the EPEC-PPP Guidance on Manual).

incurred by CAs for the replacements will be charged to the former, thereby reducing their chances to fully recover their own investments and costs. Moreover, senior lenders to EOs may also take action and apply coercive pressure for performance standards to be corrected, by stepping in and replacing the private counterpart. This opportunity to intervene is preemptive of any final decisive action by the CA to terminate the contract. In any event, in each risk-management scenario, CAs are reimbursed for any costs incurred and these costs are ultimately borne by EOs. In these cases, there is an additional element of supply risk on EOs having to ensure that the revenue/income stream matches their liabilities over the contract period. This supply risk is transferred to EOs, and it is often managed by the use of provisioning, preemptive maintenance planning, resource scheduling, product choices, seeking and maintenance of warranties, supply chain management, and so on. These management strategies are all aimed at managing many of the increased costs associated with the supply of the contract services (e.g. labor, raw materials) to ensure the supply of the asset and services—in quantity and quality—according to CAs' demand;

- *at the end of the contract (be it because of the end of its agreed duration or because of early termination)*—EOs retain significant supply risk until the end of the contract period with regard to returning the asset to CAs in the required state of maintenance and functionality, according to the contract, which may entail additional costs in order to restore assets, equipment, or other goods to the agreed state and conditions.

The Guidance Note on Directives stresses that PPP contracts must (and typically do) establish what risks are foreseeable in order to qualify as concessions. Moreover, PPP contracts must identify who is responsible in the event of such risks materializing during the execution of the contract (providing for specific consequences in case of failure to supply the contracted services to the standard defined). To this end, it is essential to contractually identify the "foreseeable, but uncertain" risks, establishing which contractual party supports the relative cost, in the event that they occur, through the preparation of a so-called *Risks Matrix*. Such a matrix is an essential tool to evaluate—at the outset and during contract performance—which specific risks have been transferred to EOs and whether such initial allocation remains throughout the whole contract duration, notwithstanding the possibility of changes in the contract provisions that may occur and are regulated for in the contract itself. In this perspective, a well-conceived availability-based PPP contract requires EOs running and exploiting works and/or services, where investments are executed and being remunerated by an availability payment, "which may be seen as a revenue stream to be exploited in the same way as a toll. In this situation it just so happens that the security for the recovery of revenue comes via a third party (i.e. the government on behalf of taxpayers), rather than directly from users (in the same way as with shadow-toll PPPs).".

Having set out this overall picture, the Guidance Note on Directives highlights that in supply/availability-based PPPs qualifying as concessions, EOs must bear the risk of a mismatch between revenues and costs due to the increase in labor costs and raw materials, interest rates, and so on. In traditional public procurement contracts, these additional costs are taken on by CAs. Conversely, in PPP contracts, ultimately, if EOs fail to manage any of the above supply risks, they could lose—or rather, not recover—their up-front investments and costs, which is the key aspect of a concession. However, in general terms, it may be difficult to judge to what extent this is simply due to mismanagement, as described in the Concessions Directive, rather than the effect of a transfer of supply risk. The outcome of this analysis will depend on a detailed perusal of the facts in each individual case. Supply/availability risk must, in fact:

- depend on external factors to EOs' organization, and
- be such as to involve, if not properly managed by EOs, the reduction of the due consideration, entailing the possibility their investments are not recouped during the execution of the contract.

In conclusion, according to the Guidance Note on Directives, the subtle and fundamental distinction between supply/availability risk and "poor management" must be analyzed and assessed on a case-by-case basis, taking into account the specific nature of the project, the characteristics of the performance required from EOs and the contractual consequences in cases of failure to reach the agreed qualitative and quantitative standards allocated to the latter.

3.4 Normal Operating Conditions and Operating Risk Versus Other Contract Risks

As mentioned, the Concessions Directive clarifies and emphasizes the notion of operating risk as the key feature of concession contracts, encompassing both the findings of the Court and further developments stemming from market practice. Therefore, the main characteristic of concession/PPP contracts—even when based on supply/availability risk—is the transfer to the concessionaire of an operating risk of an economic nature. In essence, assuming this risk, EOs, in "normal operating conditions," accept the possibility of not being able—even when complying with contractual obligations—to recoup the initial investments made and the costs subsequently incurred for carrying out the works and/or services awarded to them.

The reference to "normal operating conditions" encapsulates the correct classification of risks taken on by the concessionaire at the outset. This forecast must be taken from a predetermined and established set of data and reliable estimates, based on foreseeable events. In other words, the concession/PPP contract, although characterized by the assumption of operating risk, must not be a gamble. It must remain a contract in which the relationship between performance, verifiable events, and level of remuneration is determined ex ante, in itinere and ex post, through different monitoring instruments.

In concession contracts—when supply/availability-based risks are allocated—EOs fully assume the risks related to any increase in costs—including financial ones—necessary for the execution of the contract, and to other factors that may reduce its revenues, provided they are potentially predictable and therefore manageable. This excludes those variations deriving from an action by CAs, or from other factors, expressly envisaged and contractually regulated, such as "acts of God", which are outside the realm of "normal operating conditions.".

Uncertainty on the actual materializing of risks is required in order to qualify the contract as a concession, although *risks* should stem from a set of events *identifiable*, whilst not certain. The possible range of variables affecting concessionaires include both incurring lower costs than expected (therefore, raising the EO's revenues) and also higher costs than expected, bringing about the opposite effect. Both cases should be part of the PPP/concessions spectrum of possibilities.

In this perspective, the analysis regarding the appropriate and well-balanced transfer of operating risk must be made ex ante and must maintain a certain level of uncertainty for the EO, relating to the possible fluctuations in operating costs during the execution phase. Therefore, the possibility of recouping the investments and costs through the revenues deriving from the concession must be assessed against a factual background based on reliable data. Conversely, an ex post evaluation would lead to conceptually erroneous and paradoxical effects since it would always exclude operating risk in all cases where risks do not materialize, and/or cause disadvantageous effects for the EO, even though the same risks could have reasonably been expected to occur, at the outset. Therefore, according to this mistaken approach, the risk would end up losing its distinctive feature—which can be found in the aforementioned variability of the events connected to it—if the possibility of adverse effects actually materializing is not adequately evaluated beforehand. This background explains why a careful evaluation of risks is necessary, bearing in mind that operating risk is different from mere entrepreneurial risk, as the latter always falls on EOs, even in case of public procurement contracts. Entrepreneurial risk may, in fact, be identified with "bad management", within the meaning of the Concessions Directive and the Guidance Note on Directives because it calls on EOs' responsibility to organize its own means of production and management of resources to deliver the expected performance.

As in any other contract, EOs are free to organize all their own means (including financial ones) and the provision of services in order to maximize efficiency and economy in performing contract obligations, based on an assessment of forecast of revenues. If such forecast proves unfounded, EOs will suffer the economic consequences of flawed evaluation, but this faulty estimation does not qualify as operating risk according to the Concession Directive.

In conclusion, if compared with classic procurement contracts, the assumptions underlying PPPs and concessions are more complex and sophisticated since the transfer of operating risk entails the EOs' responsibility to ensure:

- timely execution of the works/investments, since the remuneration derives directly from the availability of the works/investment. This implies that any delay may slow down and jeopardize the prospects for recovery of the investments and costs incurred by OEs (the so-called on-time guarantee);

- quality in carrying out the works/procuring the assets, including fixed equipment and on their continued functioning according to the agreed qualitative and quantitative standards since any negligence during the investment phase may lead to higher maintenance costs, and therefore undermine the prospects of recovery for EOs (the so-called on-quality guarantee);
- management of costs, since the contractually agreed availability payment cannot be increased during contract execution, except in exceptional circumstances—which must be expressly regulated—outside the "normal operating conditions." This makes CAs' expenditure predictable and fixed (the so-called on-budget guarantee).

3.5 Operating Risk: Between the Concessions Directive and Eurostat Principles

The advantages of PPP are manifold, as it ensures both economic and timing efficiency as well as EOs' contribution to public services in terms of innovation and know-how, especially when it comes to the construction and management of infrastructure of a certain complexity or in case of services that need a series of interconnected skills and require substantial investments. However, especially in times of tight budgets, it is undeniable that CAs also appreciate being able to carry out a public project with a substantial injection of private resources as well as benefiting from the opportunity of not affecting their debt stock, even in case of infrastructure and services not paid by end-users.

Such opportunity stems from the principles set out by Eurostat, for statistical and accounting purposes, in order to obtain reliable and comparable statistics across the EU within the European system of national and regional accounts in the European Union—ESA 2010.

According to Eurostat principles—as set out in the Manual on Government Deficit and Debt (Manual)—assets involved in PPP projects can be considered non-government assets, in national accounts, and therefore "off balance-sheet", only if there is strong evidence that the private partner bears simultaneously most of the risks and rewards attached to the assets themselves (directly and linked to its use). The Manual considers that bearing such risks implies "to be entitled to take actions in order to prevent them or mitigate their impact."

As a general principle, the assets concerned are considered "off balance-sheet" for CAs if EOs bear:

- the construction risks, covering events like late delivery, respect of specifications, and increased costs;
- one of either availability—covering the volume and the quality of output (linked to the performance of the partner)—or demand risk—covering the variability of demand (the effective use of the asset by end-users)—as set in the contract, or both.

The above principles are remarkably similar to the concept of operating risk, stemming from the Court's case law and, further, implemented in the Concessions Directive.

However, the two different set of regulations should not be confused, not only because they have a different rationale, but also because there are fundamental differences between these two different regulatory rules. These important nuances should not be underestimated when contemplating setting up a PPP. In particular:

- the notion of PPP used by Eurostat and the Manual only concerns contracts where end-users do not pay directly (i.e. in a way proportional to the use of the asset and clearly identified only for this use), or if they pay, it is only for a minor part, for the use of the assets and the related services. This implies the EOs' remuneration is mainly paid for by CAs. Furthermore, for Eurostat, the concept of concession only includes contracts for the construction of assets whose use is paid directly by end-users. Conversely, as already explained, such distinction is irrelevant in the Concessions Directive;
- in the context of PPPs, Eurostat principles require the transfer of the construction risk. Conversely, the Concessions Directive does not distinguish between works and service concessions and does not consider the presence of works or assets as a qualifying element of these types of contracts. In fact, one of the major innovations of the Concessions Directive is the introduction of a single set of rules applying to both works and services concessions plus acknowledging equal standing to the different types of operating risk, that is, supply- and demand-based;

- contrary to Eurostat classifications, according to the Concessions Directive, the concept of operating risk covers all types of investments and costs that may be incurred by EOs, indistinctly, as it is linked to the concrete possibility—also known as risk—for EOs of not recovering them, or rather, the lack of any guarantee on their recovery. The Concessions Directive does not expressly mention availability risk, limiting itself to referring to a generic "supply" risk. As for the transfer of substantial operating risk, the latter may be linked to works and/or services, regardless of its qualification as construction, availability (supply), or demand, and independently from the subject matter of the contract or the amount of the related investment.

In light of the above, it should be concluded that the criteria developed by Eurostat for accounting purposes cannot be used, as such, for assessing the presence of an operating risk as required by the Concessions Directive. The Concessions Directive has a broader scope than the Manual, but, at the same time, is very strict in assessing the legal conditions evidencing the actual transfer of a substantial risk of suffering losses.

Nevertheless, some of the indications provided for in the Manual may prove useful in order to analyze individual PPP contracts with a view to assessing specific contractual arrangements and clauses from an accounting perspective, in order to verify potential issues that may prevent a proper transfer of risks to EOs (Box 3.2).[20]

Box 3.2 Assessment of PPPS from a policy perspective

From a policy perspective, apart from the European Union, at international level, other institutions have also been engaged in outlining the main features of PPPs.

For instance, the OECD, in the Recommendation of the Council on Principles for Public Governance of Public-Private Partnerships (May 2012), defines PPPs as "long-term contractual arrangements between the government and a private partner whereby the latter

(*continued*)

[20] For a thorough examination of the implications of certain typical PPP contract clauses, refer to the EPEC-PPP Guidance on Manual.

Box 3.2 (continued)

delivers and funds public services using a capital asset, sharing the associated risks". The Recommendation also stresses that in PPP contracts "the service delivery objectives of the government are intended to be aligned with the profit objectives of the private partner. The effectiveness of the alignment depends on a sufficient and appropriate transfer of risk to the private partners. In a PPP contract, the government specifies the quality and quantity of the service it requires from the private partner." In return for the service, "The private partner will receive either a stream of payments from the government for services provided or at least made available, user charges levied directly on the end users, or a combination of both".

The OECD Recommendation acknowledges that PPPs "are increasingly becoming a prominent method for delivering key public services, can deliver value for money transparently and prudently in so far as the right institutional capacities and processes are in place." Therefore, OECD recommends that the "public governance framework for Public-Private Partnerships should be set and monitored at the highest political level, so that a whole of government approach ensures affordability, transparency and value for money".

From an accounting perspective, Regulation (EU) No 549/2013 of the European Parliament and of the Council of 21 May 2013, setting up the revised European system of national and regional accounts in the European Union (ESA 2010), defines PPPs in chapter 15 as "long-term contracts between two units, whereby one unit acquires or builds an asset or set of assets, operates it for a period and then hands the asset over to a second unit. Such arrangements are usually between a private enterprise and government but other combinations are possible, with a public corporation as either party or a private NPI ['non-profit institution'] as the second party".

The ESA 2010 Regulation also describes the main reasons why CAs find it advantageous to engage in PPPs, such as: "the hope that private managements will lead to more efficient production and that access to a broader range of financial sources can be obtained and the wish to reduce government debt". Regarding the accounting aspects, the same ESA 2010 Regulation specifies that "In the contract period the PPP contractor has the legal ownership. Once the contract period is over, the government has both economic and legal ownership".

3.6 Brief Notes on Procedural Aspects

The correct qualification of PPPs as concession contracts is of particular relevance also because of its procedural consequences. Since a well-conceived PPP contract—that is, whereby the appropriate type of risk is transferred on the EO—qualifies as a concession, as a general rule, PPPs can be awarded through the more flexible procedures provided for by the Concessions Directive, contrary to the more stringent procedures envisaged by the Public Contracts Directive. The Concessions Directive defines a minimalistic procedural framework for the awarding of these contracts. In fact, with regard to award procedures, the Concessions Directive does not provide for, nor does it regulate, any specific procedure. This leaves ample room for maneuver for Member States—and for CAs, consequently—for organizing procedures in the most appropriate way, tailored to the specific contract contents.

Article 30 of the Concessions Directive expressly provides that "The contracting authority or contracting entity shall have the freedom to organise the procedure leading to the choice of concessionaire subject to compliance with this Directive". This provision has a highly innovative scope since it is the first time that an EU directive on public contracts avoids prescriptive rules on procedural models. However, it should be noted that, on the one hand, procedural freedom must be exercised by CAs in compliance with the principles—as elaborated in the procurement and concessions sector, by the EU Court (see Box 3.3)—(Principles) and, on the other hand, that the Concessions Directive prescribes a core of minimum procedural guarantees, aimed at implementing the aforementioned Principles, to ensure transparency, equal treatment, proportionality and mutual recognition are always respected in the launching and conducting of awarding procedures as well as in the execution of the ensuing contracts.

To conclude the Concessions Directive affords CAs' wide procedural freedom, allowing them to explore all forms of dialogue and negotiation compatible and in compliance with the Principles, with particular reference to the prescriptions set by Article 3 of the Concessions Directive, which specifically requires CAs:

- to treat EOs equally and without discrimination and act in a transparent and proportionate manner;
- not to conceive the concession award procedure, including the estimate of the value, with the intention of excluding it from the scope

Box 3.3 The principles

The Principles were developed by the Court in relation to public contracts. They are applicable to both public procurement contracts and concessions, as both contracts fall under the general EU Internal Market legislative framework, which aims at ensuring free movement of goods and services by removing any obstacles based on national protectionism and implementing the general principle of non-discrimination on the basis of nationality. The Principles are aimed at ensuring the achievement of the main objectives of EU procurement—and concessions—policy: the opening of national procurement markets to all products, services, and EOs without discrimination or limitations that could hinder the widest possible participation, on an equal footing, while ensuring effective competition, resulting in better and more convenient offers for CAs.

The main applicable Principles are:

- equal treatment—which translates into ensuring, in the context of awarding procedures, the same objective conditions for all EOs wishing to be awarded the contract, including those not participating in the procedures who may be interested should the specific conditions be different. During contract execution, the principle of equal treatment implies that terms and conditions of the contract, as well as its scope, cannot be modified substantially (see Chap. 4);
- transparency (corollary of equal treatment)—which means ensuring adequate, clear, and unambiguous publicity of all the relevant elements concerning the awarding of the contract, so as to allow informed participation and avoid any arbitrariness in the conduct of the procedures. Transparency is also required in relation to communications, reasoning, and access to documents, in order to allow interested parties to challenge adverse decisions before the competent judge;
- proportionality—that is the need not to restrict market access to a greater extent than is strictly necessary to achieve the expected result. This principle is expressed, above all, in the setting of requirements for selecting bidders and evaluating

(*continued*)

Box 3.3 (continued)

offers, as well as concerning possible conditions upon the performance of contracts. All of those—though allowed—must be objective and proportionate *vis-à-vis* the subject matter and scope of the contract to be awarded;

- mutual recognition—that is the obligation to accept authorized products and services (technical specifications)—as well as professional qualifications obtained—in other Member States, without limiting their scope or questioning their validity.

The above Principles act as a boundary—but, at the same time, as a stimulus and instrument—to establish the correct synthesis of the opposite needs of CAs, on one hand, and EOs, on the other, not only when choosing the counterpart, but also when executing the contract.

To ensure compliance with the principles, correct ex ante planning of the operation—not only in its procedural performance, but also in the previous phase of collecting the needs, that is, appropriate identification of the scope of the contract—is the best guarantee to ensure that the principles and rules are complied with, during the awarding procedure and contract execution. Furthermore, in full compliance with the above principles, correct planning and structuring of the overall operation allow for the provision of the appropriate measures so as to ensure the correct execution of the contract over time, attempting to prevent the need to abort the project and/or re-negotiate the contract (see Chap. 4).

of the Concessions Directive or of unduly favoring or disadvantaging certain EOs or certain works, supplies, or services;

- to aim at ensuring the transparency of the award procedure and of the performance of the contract in compliance with the confidentiality requirements, pursuant to article 28 of the Concessions Directive.

Finally, it should be noted that procedural requirements—other than the Principles—must be seen as a tool to ensure appropriateness of the contract: in other words, they are just functional to satisfy CAs' needs. This approach has been further stressed by the EU Commission in the wake of the Covid-19 pandemic. The "Guidance from the European Commission on using the public procurement framework in the emergency situation related to the COVID-19 crisis"[21] was issued by the Commission to implement operational guidelines in order to foster emergency-related procurement and, at the same time, to remind Member States and CAs of the importance of programming their procurement carefully so as to provide swiftly to their increasing needs.

The Commission highlights that EU public procurement framework provides all necessary flexibility to public buyers to purchase goods and services directly linked to the COVID-19 crisis as quickly as possible. This also involves more accomplished methodologies to engage in interaction with EOs, taking into account also strategic aspects, like environmental, innovative, and social requirements, including accessibility to any services procured, that can be integrated in public procurement processes. All in all, apart from the possibility to use emergency direct procedures—which must be justified by unforeseeable events not attributable to CAs, such as the pandemic—the Commission's strategic message is that procedural rules contain the necessary flexibility so as to accommodate public needs, in the context of major and disastrous events, but also on a more stable basis. CAs should take advantage of such flexibility, so as to be more efficient and effective in their buying strategies. On a different level, this also means CAs should be aware of all tools available to them, including contract models different from traditional procurement—such as concessions/PPPs—and should not hesitate to use them, when appropriate, especially if they can guarantee better results.

[21] Communication from the Commission (2020/C 108 I/01), published on OJEU C 108 I/01, 1.04.2020.

CHAPTER 4

PPP Contracts and Features

Veronica Vecchi and Velia M. Leone

Abstract This chapter analyzes the two PPP contracts for infrastructure and service delivery, the user fee-based PPP and availability-based PPP; it also presents and discusses build, lease, and transfer (BLT) contracts as a minor form of PPP. Further it sheds the light on some of the most important elements that need to be considered when structuring PPP contracts, such as: payment mechanisms, contract duration, systems of deductions/penalties to ensure appropriate incentives to SPVs, and how to link payments to inflation. This chapter also discusses the renegotiation of PPP contracts under a legal perspective.

Keywords Tariff-based PPP • Availability-based PPP • Indexation to inflation • PPP light • BLT

4.1 Introduction

PPP contracts are usually set up according to one of the two main models, namely one based on fees paid by end-users or the other one based on an availability payment by contracting authorities (CAs). User fee-based contracts, as described in Chap. 1, are internationally known as BOT, even though they should be more accurately defined as (DF)BOT—(Design, Finance), Build, Operate, Transfer. Availability-based contracts are known

V. Vecchi et al., *Public Private Partnerships*,
https://doi.org/10.1007/978-3-030-65435-1_4

as DBFMO—Design, Build, Finance, Maintain, and Operate. Since many acronyms have been used across the world to identify different models of PPP contracts, and considering that PPP contracts should be deeply customized according to the specific needs of the particular CA and the relevant context, we deem it better to refer to the two macro-categories, namely "user fee-based PPP" and "availability-based PPP."

The user fee-based contract is often defined as a concession, that is, the classic legal model underpinning this type of contract. However, since a well-balanced PPP contract depends on technical (design, construction, service), economic, and financial, as well as, but not restricted to, legal issues, in this chapter, we refrain from referring to legal terminologies, while dealing with the legal dimension of PPP procurement separately (see Chap. 3). Furthermore, since legal frameworks are different across the world, it is better to avoid legal classifications when discussing PPP contractual features common to the entire international business community.

Traditionally, user fee-based PPPs were applied to transactions concerning economic infrastructure, whilst availability-based PPPs were introduced in the UK, under the so-called PFI (Private Finance Initiative) policy, in order to build and operate social infrastructure, such as schools, hospitals, and prisons. However, in recent years, policies have evolved, and availability-based PPPs have also been used for economic infrastructure, especially in markets where demand is very volatile, or unpredictable, as discussed in Chap. 1.

That said, however, in general, other contract models may also be considered PPPs. Among those, for example, the so-called Turnkey contracts, such as Design, Build, and Finance (DBF) and Build and Finance (BF), where the private partner—usually an EPC (Engineer, Procure, and Construct) company—is in charge of financing (designing) and building a new infrastructure, or refurbishing an existing one. Typically, the EPC company is paid, once works are completed, through a lump sum payment. Therefore, capital costs also include the cost of financing (rolled-up interests) raised by the EPC company to finance its investment. A similar model is the so-called Build, Lease, and Transfer (BLT), where CAs pay the investment through leasing instalments over a 10–20-year period. In BLT contracts, the counterpart is generally a consortium formed by an EPC company and a financial institution. This book does not specifically dwell on Design and Finance (DF) and Design, Build, and Finance (DBF), since, from a legal standpoint, they are de facto very similar to traditional procurement contracts. This is the case notwithstanding the fact that, when well structured, they allow for allocation of on-time and on-budget risks. Conversely, a specific paragraph deals with BLT models since, in some countries, they are used as a simpler form of PPP, especially to deliver on-time and on-budget investments.

This chapter analyzes some of the most important elements that need to be considered when structuring PPP contracts. In particular, the following topics are discussed: payment mechanisms in user fee-based and availability-based PPPs, contract duration, systems of deductions/penalties to ensure appropriate incentives to SPVs, and how to link payments to inflation. Risk allocation, the most peculiar feature of PPP, is discussed in Chap. 5.

4.2 User Fee-Based PPP

As previously mentioned, this type of PPP is mainly used for economic infrastructure, that is, those contracts meant to deliver services paid by end-users. It is worth noting that this type of infrastructure is called economic because it can be economically exploited: in other words, it can be used to deliver services paid by end-users, through tariffs, which remunerate the private investments. Across the world, it is common practice to involve market players in the management of such services, as discussed in Chap. 1, in order to achieve higher levels of efficiency and effectiveness. Some examples include: building/revamping and operating motorways, carparks, sports facilities, tramways and subways, ports, logistic hubs, waste treatment plants, water sanitation and distribution plants, energy production, storage and distribution plants.

In such contracts, since the only source of revenue consists of tariffs paid by end-users, economic operators (EOs) bear all or most of the demand risks, although such risks may be mitigated by the CA through various types of guarantees, such as minimum revenue guarantee, as discussed in Chap. 2.

This type of contract faces some critical issues, especially when applied to greenfield infrastructure, where demand can be difficult to forecast. The unpredictability of demand can affect the feasibility and bankability of the project. Demand risk is easier to estimate in brownfield projects. Unpredictable demand may have a lesser impact on projects with minor investment components, where the main goal of PPP contracts is the delivery of intangible services. In this case, tariffs are mainly meant for remuneration of operational costs.

When demand is difficult to estimate, it is advisable to structure PPP contracts relying on availability charges, whereby the demand risk is retained by CAs. The latter can use the tariffs collected (often by the SPV) to fund availability payments. After the so-called ramp-up phase, that is, a transition period after the construction phase, as soon as revenues are more stable and it is possible to establish demand trends through a statistical method based on historical series, the payment mechanism can be switched to a tariff regime. At this stage, in general, demand is more predictable and, therefore, relative risks are quite similar to brownfield projects. The choice of basing PPP contracts on availability payments is further justified by considering that, in a well-structured contract, only those risks that can be controlled and influenced by EOs should be transferred to them. Indeed, for large infrastructure, especially when greenfield, not only is demand difficult to estimate but also it cannot be easily influenced by EOs through its management activities because it mainly depends on macroeconomic and social factors (see Box 4.1).

Box 4.1 Examples: availability payment in motorways
A11 motorway, Belgium

A DBFMO contract was chosen by the Flemish Agency for Roads and Traffic to design, finance, build, maintain, and operate the A11 motorway, in the surroundings of Bruges, in the Flanders region. The project was awarded in 2012. The 33.5-year contract, of which 3.5 years were for construction, presents some peculiarities. Apart from being one of the first motorway projects in Europe to be structured as a DBFMO contract, that is, providing for a remuneration structure based on an availability charge, it is also characterized by a public-private SPV, in which a public-owned limited company, Via Invest NV, owns 39.33% of the shares. Via Invest is a joint venture established in 2006 between the Flemish Transport Authority AWV and Participatiemaatschappij Vlaanderen (PMV), an independent investment company owned by the Flemish government to support the economic development of Flanders.

Further, the A11 project raised 88% of the required capital from capital markets, through a project bond. The project was made more appealing for bondholders, not only by the fact that demand risk was

(*continued*)

Box 4.1 (continued)

retained by the authority, but, also, thanks to the provision of a guarantee by the European Investment Bank (EIB) through an unfunded project bond credit enhancement (PBCE) facility. Such a facility takes the form of a letter of credit, covering 20% of the senior debt during the construction phase. That can be used in order to provide liquidity in the event that cash flow generated by the project is not sufficient to ensure senior bond debt service or to cover construction costs. After completion of the construction phase, the maximum amount secured by the letter of credit steps down to 10% of the bonds. Despite the presence of an availability-based payment, the project rating would have been Baa3 in Moody's view. Thanks to the involvement of the PBCE from the EIB, the rating of the bonds was enhanced by three notches, receiving a definitive A3 senior secured rating.

Source: Vecchi et al. (2015)

Pedemontana Veneta, Italy

This is another interesting case, where the availability payment was introduced as a consequence of the contract renegotiation, carried out in 2017–2018, with the aim to exclude the previously provided minimum revenue guarantee, which, if triggered, would have been extremely expensive for the regional authority, with an estimated disbursement of €14 billion. The latter was calculated as the difference between the forecasted revenues in the financial plan of the PPP and the revenues calculated according to more accurate estimates based on actual demand.

The original contract, signed in 2009, was based on a capital investment of €1.8 billion, to be mainly financed by the SPV, with a small capital grant of €174 million to be paid by the region. The economic and financial equilibrium was based on (1) revenues from tolls, estimated on the basis of generous traffic forecasts, probably to reduce the amount of public grant needed, and (2) an additional availability payment across 30 years of €14.5 million each year (totaling €18 billion). In 2013, the contract was renegotiated for the first time, as a consequence of an increase in capital costs (up to €2.2 billion). The renegotiation increased the amount of grant by €600 million and the payment of €18 billion of availability charges was concentrated in the first 15 years of the management phase.

(continued)

Box 4.1 (continued)

The initially overestimated demand forecast had prevented some of the main development banks operating in Italy from financing the project: the lack of confidence demonstrated by such anchor investors had de facto made the project unbankable. Considering that works had already started, thus making it impossible, or at least unacceptable, to terminate the project without seriously harming public interest, the authority entered into a process of close scrutiny of the contract not only to find a sound solution for the SPV to be able to issue a project bond, but also to make the contract affordable for taxpayers while ensuring its compliance with EU and national laws. The solution found was to shift the payment mechanism, from demand-based to availability-based, by excluding the SPV from risks (and revenues) deriving from demand. Actually, demand risk was already virtually retained by the regional authority, anyway, because of the potentially expensive minimum revenue guarantee. The capital grant was increased by €300 million, borrowed by the region from the national development bank.

The availability payment was determined so as to match the tolls collected and retained by the authority. Since a stable payment and an increased capital grant allowed a reduction by almost 50% of the revenues needed to achieve the expected return, through the renegotiation of the contract, the SPV accepted a slight reduction in the return of the project. At the same time, the region benefited from a more stable prospect and a significant reduction of its potential risks, as well as a stronger commitment by the SPV to deliver high-quality and reliable services. Similarly to the A11 project, the availability payment is only partially linked to the inflation (see Sect. 4.5 for an explanation of such feature). The availability payment is subject to deductions and penalties in order to ensure sound risk allocation and appropriate incentives to make certain the infrastructure is well managed and maintained according to predefined quality standards.

Overall, the renegotiation allowed the region to cancel the minimum revenue mechanism that would have exposed the regional budget to a likely payment of €14 billion. The new and more conservative traffic estimates would be able to ensure the collection of tolls for an amount sufficient to cover not only availability payments but also the debt service toward the development bank.

Source: Official documents of Regione del Veneto and Delibera ANAC n. 1202—22 November 2017

When availability charge is applied, it is fundamental to ensure other risks, such as construction and service performance, are appropriately allocated. To this end, adequate deductions and/or penalties should be applied to the availability payment when service standards are not met, from a quantitative and/or qualitative standpoint. However, sound contract monitoring, based on key performance indicators, should also be put in place when the payment mechanism is based on tariffs, charged directly to end-users, since many economic infrastructures have a rigid demand, due to their characteristics as a natural monopoly. In these instances, the quality of services does not drive the demand and EOs may fail to deliver the expected quality with, potentially, lesser effect on the project revenues.

The payment to the EO may also be shaped as a shadow toll, whereby CAs pay EOs per each single user, without effectively charging end-users. However, this form of payment does not address the lack of predictability of the demand since demand risk is retained by EOs. This form of indirect tolling is, therefore, chosen for policy reasons by those authorities who are willing to allow end-users' access to relevant infrastructure and services free of charge. The shadow toll system has mostly been applied to transport infrastructure projects.

Demand forecast is even more difficult in emerging countries, where people are not used to paying a fee for services and the majority of the population may prefer to continue to use old infrastructure; this is quite common for transport infrastructures. In such contexts, CAs may choose to apply lower tariffs to accustom people progressively to paying tariffs. Such choice entails the need for CAs to integrate EOs' revenues from fees with additional resources collected through general taxation.

When demand is difficult to estimate, the use of a revenue-sharing mechanism is another option to consider. This is, usually, applied when revenues are generous and forecasted returns of the project are likely to be higher than the optimal level of return as pre-determined on the basis of the level of transferred risks. In the case of hard-to-be-predicted demand, CAs can choose to structure a PPP contract based on a conservative estimate of demand and to support it with a capital grant. In such cases, including a revenue-sharing mechanism in the contract allows for adjustment should revenues increase to a level above the set ceiling, by "clawing back" the excess, thus generating a sort of "remuneration" of the initial grant paid by CAs. The revenue-sharing mechanism should be triggered by increased revenues above a certain level, to be defined prior to the awarding procedure or the closing of the contract, on the basis of a sensitivity analysis of financial plan. In such cases, it is fundamental to put in place a transparent mechanism of revenue/demand monitoring. Sometimes, CAs are not keen on granting revenue or capital contributions or tariff integrations to EOs, for budgetary constraints or for fear of sanctions from audit authorities, thus preferring to extend contract duration. However, this approach is wrong since it is not based on solid financial evaluations. When the gross margin (i.e. the difference between revenues and operational expenses) of a PPP project is limited, the achievement of financial equilibrium would, in fact, require an excessive extension of the contract duration, which, in turn, may provoke a de facto monopoly. Furthermore, an abnormally long contract duration would not be consistent with the average length of financial contracts, which is generally set between 10 and 20 years. A longer maturity period is possible only where a development bank is part of the financial jigsaw of the deal. Therefore, the need to match contract duration with debt maturity requires entering a debt renegotiation: this is a risk EOs are rarely willing to bear.

Demand risk may prove difficult to manage not only in case of endogenous demand rigidity or demand unpredictability, but also when CAs make the demand rigid as a consequence of certain policy goals to be achieved. For example, if CAs are willing to promote equity, through generalized and equal access to critical services, a remunerative tariff, that is, a tariff covering operational cost, capital cost, and the cost of financial resources invested by EOs, is not appropriate or may not be affordable by end-users and, therefore, an availability mechanism should be preferred.

Also, if CAs decide to provide social tariffs for some categories of users, such as the young or the elderly, sometimes associated with specific service requirements (e.g. in sports facilities CAs often require services and tariffs to be set so as to encourage certain categories of users, such as students or sports associations), a revenue integration could be a sound option. Revenue integration mechanism should be adequately crafted. Such mechanism may provide for tariff integrations—that is, an integration for each tariff paid by specific categories of end-users in order to reach the level of remuneration needed for the project to be sustainable—thus leaving demand risk with EOs, or it can take the form of a fixed revenue integration to be calculated on the basis of the financial plan. The latter solution should be preferred when specific policy goals heavily influence the revenues structure, thus limiting EOs' room for maneuver.

Lastly, CAs may opt to allow EOs' access to commercial revenues in order to sustain an infrastructure project with a weak demand. Such a solution should be carefully explored since it may increase the complexity of the project, thus requiring the execution of the contract by a consortium of EOs with multiple competencies.

4.3 Availability-based PPP

As already mentioned, availability-based PPPs—setting aside the above suggestions regarding economic infrastructure in cases where demand is unpredictable or greatly impacted by policy choices—are usually appropriate for projects aimed at delivering:

1. infrastructure or investments needed for the delivery of services directly operated by public authorities, as it may be the case for some critical services, such as health or education. These are also considered merit goods, that is, services ensuring great public benefits and, therefore, are generally funded with general taxation, especially because tariffs may not be affordable for the majority of the population;
2. general public services, when tariffs cannot be applied because they are provided on a communal basis, as opposed to services provided to a specific target of users (for this reason general public services are considered public good, which are defined by the economic theory as non-excludable and non-rivalrous). These are, therefore, funded by general taxation, such as street lighting or urban facility management;
3. infrastructures used by public authorities (office buildings or facilities in the defense sector); and
4. non-core services bought by authorities, such as energy management.

In such transactions, EOs are in charge of design, financing, and building of infrastructure and delivery of so-called non-core services. The availability charge is set so as to ensure the remuneration of operational costs, capital costs, and costs of the private capital invested. Payment of the availability charge is ensured by CAs through public resources deriving from general taxation.

When PPP contracts involve infrastructure for the delivery of merit goods, such as schools and hospitals, availability charges generally ensure the remuneration of investment and infrastructure maintenance (hard-facility management costs); all other possible services, to be included in the contract, are usually paid via specific tariffs, sometimes even based on consumption, though minimum quantities are generally provided for in the contract.

In such cases, it is advisable to avoid extending the scope of contracts, by including too many services, and a light model should be preferred in order to avoid excessive complexity (see Box 4.2). This is even more the case as non-core services tend to evolve rapidly and their quick evolution is difficult to contractualize while maintaining balanced risk allocation. In emerging countries, however, the main trend is to include many non-core services in the scope of the contract, aspiring to reach wider or even complete outsourcing. This approach is based on the assumption that private

Box 4.2 PPP light

In the "light" PPP model, SPVs are entrusted with design, financing, and building of non-economic facilities (such as schools and hospitals), and with the technical management thereof, namely with hard-facility services only, that is, those strictly related to the availability of the newly built facility. The rationale of such a "light model" is that only those services strictly related to the core and main investments shall be included in PPP contracts. Therefore, for example, if a hospital authority needs the renewal of medical equipment (investment component), the management component of the contract should include only those services related to the underlying investment, that is, the maintenance and renewal of equipment. In this case, the contract may also include the delivery of supporting services when relevant to the performance of the main service through nurses or specialized technicians, who would support and work under the clinical governance of the health authority.

The "light model" allows CAs to avoid many of the drawbacks present in overly extended contracts, such as the following ones.

- Rigidity and benchmarking clauses. Including many non-core services within the scope of an availability-based PPP contract may induce rigidity in future decisions of CAs. This is because prices and delivery modes of non-core services, as well as the needs of CAs, may change significantly during contract life. In the healthcare sector, for example, de-hospitalization trends lead to the

(*continued*)

Box 4.2 (continued)

progressive reduction of hospital capacity and length of stay. This implies that non-core services should be modified accordingly. The same happens in the education sector, where new technologies, but also disruptive events such as those observed during the Covid-19 pandemic, can change service requirements. In order to avoid rigidity, many of such contracts provide for benchmarking clauses. In principle, such clauses, aimed at renegotiating the scope and price of non-core services, have proven ineffective in granting the flexibility needed to update contractual conditions. This is because, traditionally, they have been solely conceived as a way to reduce fees for services in order to achieve spending review targets. The benchmark test methodology, currently applied to many contracts, is based on the calculation of an average price, on the assumption that it should capture market price. The latter may be defined on the basis of a representative number of bids collected by CAs, a new offer submitted by the SPV, and an official benchmark, such as a standard price released by national authorities or observatories. If the resulting average price falls within a certain price-band, generally within a range of +/-10%, the price of the service involved does not need to be rectified. Otherwise, provided it does not appear anomalous, the price of the contract service has to be modified accordingly. This methodology may induce the EOs and SPVs to adopt moral hazard behaviors. This is because EOs, not part of the contract, only have to provide offers, but they are not committed because, at a later stage, the SPV will not involve them in the delivery of the service. Therefore, such players may be tempted to offer below-market prices in order to try and reduce the SPV's marginalities so as to undermine their competitors. On the other hand, the same mechanism may induce SPVs to offer higher prices in order to keep the average price within the initial range and thus avoiding price reductions.

- Indexation. When service fees, generally fully indexed to inflation rates, are designed so as to remunerate also the investment component, there is a risk of over-indexation. This can undermine value for money and affordability of the project. The indexation

(*continued*)

Box 4.2 (continued)

mechanism may also expose SPVs to the risk of under-profitability if actual inflation rate is lower than forecasted in the financial plan. In the latter case, however, SPVs are generally protected since the contract can be renegotiated. However, the indexation mechanism is complex to manage. For instance, if CAs renegotiate the contract using the wrong method, this can cause an extra payment to the SPV.

- Overpricing. When multiple non-core services are included and the main SPV shareholders are industrial players, as is often the case, in a context of low competition due to the complexity of PPP transactions, the risk of over-estimated services prices is high, thus increasing extra-profitability for the SPV. To explain how the extra-profitability is generated, an example proves useful. In one project, upon scrutiny by the competent Audit Authority, it was found that the annual overall difference between the costs for non-core services in comparable hospitals and the unitary payment due (which, in that case, was calculated as the sum of service fees since the contract did not include an availability charge) was about €25–26 million. Considering that production costs for PPP and traditional contracts are similar (even though, generally, SPVs are able to get more favorable prices from subcontracts than healthcare organizations entering traditional procurement contracts), this difference can be considered as the remuneration for the investment, thus increasing de facto the return for investors (implying a project IRR in the range 12.5% and 13%, which is far higher than that derived from the financial model annexed to the contract [6.60%]). However, it must be noted that this net margin is not wholly retained by the SPV directly, but is instead mainly passed on to subcontractors, which are also the SPV's shareholders. This case clearly draws attention because extra margins hidden in non-core services, difficult to detect and also reduced thanks to the competition during the tender phase, may generate returns that are not captured in the official financial plan of the contract.

(*continued*)

Box 4.2 (continued)

- Other possible drawbacks. The inclusion of too many non-core services in standard DBFMO contracts may also generate possible further drawbacks. First of all, it can jeopardize the market for small and medium enterprises, including those of a social nature, often involved in the delivery of non-core services, creating insurmountable entry barriers. Such EOs may not have the necessary means, especially equity, to become industrial investors and, as mere subcontractors of SPVs, they may be forced to reduce their marginalities to the benefit of industrial and financial investors. This is because they usually act as subcontractors of industrial investors, thus allowing them to extract a higher return than those officially declared in the contract. Furthermore, when the scope of the project is widened through the addition of a significant number of non-core services, the contract may turn out to be incomplete, thus enhancing the risk of contract renegotiation, with potential negative consequences in terms of affordability and value for money.
  Source: Vecchi et al. (2020)

players should be more efficient than the public sector or to avoid multiple awarding procedures, which are expensive, time consuming, and risky, especially in terms of litigation. The truth is that EOs' efficiency can be captured also by traditional, though sophisticated, contracts, while transaction costs associated with the management of such contracts are not higher than those associated with the effective management of complex PPP contracts. Therefore, the features of the contract, and, especially, the services to be included therein, must be carefully considered and designed ex ante since avoiding any misconceived emulation effect is of the essence. An important lesson to be learned is that the institutional and regulatory framework, as well as factual circumstances, do matter and although a contract model may work in a jurisdiction, this conclusion may not be true in another one.

An effective payment mechanism should be conceived as follows:

Availability Payment: investment component + maintenance component + service fees (if further services are included)

The investment component remunerates capital expenses, such as design and construction costs, and the cost of capital (debt and equity). Therefore, the actual amount of the availability payment depends on the volume of investments and duration of the contract since its aim is to achieve the economic and financial equilibrium, according to the methodology illustrated in Chap. 7.

As with user fee-based PPP, the duration of availability-based PPP contracts should also be defined on the basis of the average maturity of loans available in the financial market. In order to choose an appropriate duration for the contract, the life span of the involved technologies should also be accurately taken into account. As regards technology, it is suggested that refresh provisions should be limited to a minimum since they increase contract complexity and costs; indeed, technology refresh requires the provision of sophisticated contract clauses, in order to allow flexibility, while maintaining an adequate risk allocation. The definition of the technical and price evolution of technologies across a long-term contract might be challenging. There is a potential risk CAs may not access the best and most appropriate technologies available, at market prices. That said, it may also be difficult for EOs to accurately foresee technical and price evolution. This scenario explains the tendency to overestimate the attached risks, affecting the affordability and value for money of contracts.

Availability payment mechanisms should be associated with an adequate system of deductions and penalties in case SPVs should not be able to deliver the predefined level of availability of the facilities or meet the quality standards for services. A sound mechanism of deductions for the availability payment should be based on two different levels, that is, a minimum and an average one. Therefore, for each of the main areas of the facility involved, the contract should include minimum and average indicators, thus allowing for a granular definition of the meaning of availability and, therefore, the application of deductions/penalties. The system could, for instance, be designed in the following ways:

- if the SPV meets the average parameters, no deductions are applied;
- if the availability falls between the minimum and the average levels, to be detected and measured for each single indicator, deductions associated with each of such indicators can be applied only to the maintenance component of the payment;
- if the availability further falls below the minimum target, then deductions may also affect the investment component, thus resulting in an actual reduction of the return.

When other non-core services are included, specific key performance indicators and deductions should be applied to service fees. It is important that the amount of the deduction creates incentives for SPVs to foster a sound management of the contract. In fact, if deductions are too low, SPVs have no incentive to put in place all the measures to avoid the under-performance, because the impact of deductions/penalties on their return is lower than the cost involved in delivering the expected standards. In some cases, it may be useful for CAs to calculate the social costs generated by disruption in the availability of the facility or services: this could be a good benchmark in order to identify the appropriate level of applicable deductions/penalties.

A sound system of deductions and penalties, ensuring the appropriate risk allocation is maintained throughout the duration of the contract, is required for availability-based contracts under European Union rules in order to ensure the off-balance sheet treatment of the investment (see Chap. 5).

The payment mechanism illustrated above is typically applied to availability-based contracts in health and education. However, as written above, the need for a sound deduction/penalty system can also be applied to user fee-based PPPs when the demand is rigid and user satisfaction is not a sufficiently appropriate efficient driver to enhance the performance by the SPV.

Payment mechanisms can be conceived in a different way when PPP contracts apply to the delivery of general public services and non-core services, such as energy management of office buildings. PPP contracts for energy management are often referred to as Energy Performance Contracts. In such contracts, the authority can pay a service fee on the basis of energy consumption, which covers not only the energy used but also the investment and maintenance of the relevant appliances and systems. In standard Energy Performance Contracts, the service fee is generally set at the same level of the costs faced by CAs for energy management before the energy efficiency investment. However, it is often the case that the efficiency achieved is not sufficient to ensure remuneration of the capital invested when investments are significant. In this case, payment should be structured as follows:

Availability Payment: investment component + maintenance component + energy consumptions

4.4 Build, Lease, and Transfer

BLT contracts are sometimes used to procure investments such as schools, hospitals, complex medical equipment, and office buildings, in contexts where the main service is delivered by the authority itself. As per classic availability-based PPPs, BLT contracts allow assets to be purchased by CAs without incurring in upfront investments. Consequently, this type of contract is attractive for CAs suffering from inadequate budgets to meet capital requirements or in contexts where conservative fiscal policies impose a reduction of the level of public debt. Furthermore, because BLT contracts may be easier to structure, since they are rather similar to standard procurement contracts, they are appreciated by authorities, especially the smallest ones.

A lease is a contract between a lessee (in this case, a CA) and a lessor (an association of EOs, including, at least, an asset provider and a specialized leasing firm or a bank). The contract establishes that the authority has the right to use the specified asset, by paying periodic installments to the lessor. Periodic fees are generally fixed, as in a standard financial contract. Therefore, the leasing structure provides a de facto guarantee on payments from CAs to the leasing company, thus providing additional comfort to lenders. As a consequence, debt providers apply a lower interest rate to lease contracts concluded with the public sector, compared to traditional PPP contracts, where the borrowers are SPVs, whose rating (or, rather, the project rating) is lower. This entails leasing fees being, usually, more affordable than standard availability charges. However, to achieve the same advantages of availability-based PPP contracts, the BLT contract should be conceived so as to fully allocate the availability risk on the lessor through a system of deductions and penalties, as explained in Sect. 4.3.

To fully understand how to structure a BLT contract, it is important to appreciate the differences between finance leases and operating leases. The difference between the two models lies with the economic ownership of the asset, based on the allocation of the relevant "risks and rewards." In finance leases, CAs retain the so-called economic ownership of the asset (which means all the risks associated with ownership, maintenance in particular) and the lessors' role is equivalent to that of a debt providers. In this case, public deficit and debt are impacted for the full value of the assets at the time CAs take possession thereof, namely as soon as CAs can use the asset. By contrast, an operating lease implies no ownership transfer to the lessee, and the risks and rewards typical of economic ownership (such as designing and constructing the asset, along with insuring and maintaining it) are kept on the private sector lessor's balance-sheet. In this case, lease fees paid by CAs can be regarded as current expenses and the deficit and debt impact of investment are spread over the duration of the contract. In conclusion, BLT contracts can be regarded as PPP contracts only if they are structured as operating leases, able to ensure that not only on-time and on-budget goals are achieved, but also to guarantee the quality of the investment (i.e. the availability).

4.5 How to Link PPP Payments to Inflation

When structuring the payment mechanism of PPP contracts, of any kind, indexation to inflation rate is always a critical element to consider carefully. Indexation is important in long-term contracts in order to ensure revenues maintain the purchasing power needed to cover operating costs throughout their entire duration. However, when the project involves significant investments, the majority of revenues is committed to covering capital expenses and the cost of debt, which, as a general rule, are both fixed. Actually, investment costs included in the financial plan may already incorporate the estimated inflation, at least in mature economies where inflation is quite stable and predictable. Therefore, only the part of revenues intended to cover operating costs and equity remuneration should be linked to inflation. Inflation assumptions incorporated in the financial plan of the project might result in being quite different from actual inflation, used to index tolls and availability payments during contract execution. In this context, if the entire revenues provided for in the contract are linked to inflation, project returns may change significantly, thus exposing both parties to a risk that they cannot control, as is shown in Table 4.1. If actual inflation is lower than predicted, revenues will grow at a slower pace, thus generating a contraction of the return; if, on the contrary, actual inflation is higher than predicted, revenues will grow more rapidly, thus generating a higher profitability. By reducing the amount of revenues linked to the inflation, a higher portion thereof has to be forecasted in the financial plan, at least in the first years of the management phase. This can be a critical issue; however, partial indexation is fundamental in order to reduce the return volatility, thereby limiting the risk of contract renegotiation. Furthermore, the suggested approach is also useful to reduce the overall amount of revenues needed to secure the target return, improving the value for money for taxpayers and the affordability of availability-based PPPs for CAs. The latter is shown in Table 4.2.

Table 4.1 Impact of the inflation on contract return (measured through the net present value) when revenues are partially or totally linked to inflation

Forecasted and actual inflation	*50% of revenues are linked to inflation. Figures in local currency (revenues at year 0:531)*	*Revenues fully linked to inflation. Figures in local currency (revenues at year 0:456)*
	Ex ante NPV	
Forecasted inflation in the economic-financial plan: 10%	74	74
	Ex ante NPV	
Actual inflation: 7% (lower than forecasted)	27	-1.8
Actual inflation: 15% (higher than forecasted)	60	218

Table 4.2 Impact of the inflation indexation on the availability charge for a contract with a capital investment of 100 million and a forecasted inflation at 2%

Availability charge (AC)	*40% of the AC is linked to the inflation (in local currency)*	*100% of the AC is linked to the inflation (in local currency)*
AC at year 0	17.5 million	16.2 million
Total ACs across the contract	445 million	460 million
Present value of ACs across the contract	282 million	288 million

4.6 Modifications and Re-negotiation of PPP Contracts: A Legal Perspective

From a legal standpoint, it is possible to modify the conditions of a PPP contract, during its execution, only if the following two main requirements are satisfied, namely:

- on one hand, the CAs' power to impose certain changes, for reasons relating to public interest. These CAs' prerogative emphasizes EOs obligations to abide by CAs' requirements, provided the total amount of the requested changes is below certain threshold values;
- on the other hand, to avoid distortion of competition, to ensure equal treatment and a level playing field for actual and potential competitors. These prerequisites limit CAs' power to modify the original conditions

> upon which initial competition was solicited, that is, the awarding procedure. In particular, under EU legal framework, CAs must ensure equal treatment and transparency in the awarding procedure. The abidance to these principles also implies initial conditions requested during the awarding phase cannot be modified by entering into a (new) contract featuring elements not requested during the procedure, or by substantially modifying the same contract during its performance. In this perspective, any substantial modification of a contract in execution is equivalent to the (direct) negotiation of a new contract.

The EU Court of Justice case law provides interpretative guidance to determine whether the changes to a given contract should be considered substantial, within the meaning of EU legal framework (refer to Chap. 3 for a description of the most relevant features of the EU Directive on concessions) and, therefore, trigger a new award. According to the EU Court case-law,[1] the "amendments to the provisions of a public contract during the currency of the contract constitute a new award of a contract [...] when they are materially different in character from the original contract and, therefore, such as to demonstrate the intention of the parties to renegotiate the essential terms of that contracts." It follows that the modification of a contract can be considered "material":

- when it introduces conditions which, had they been part of the initial award procedure, would have allowed for the admission of tenderers other than those initially admitted or would have allowed for the acceptance of a tender other than the one initially accepted, or
- when it extends the scope of the contract considerably to encompass services not initially covered, or, again
- when it changes the economic balance of the contract in favor of the contractor in a manner which was not provided for in the terms and conditions of the initial contract.

The EU Court also specified[2] that "the very fact that, because of their subject matter, certain public contracts may immediately be categorised as being unpredictable in nature means that there is a foreseeable risk that difficulties may occur at the implementation stage. Accordingly, in respect

[1] Judgment of the Court, 19 June 2008, C-454/06, Pressetext.
[2] Judgment of the Court, 7 September 2016, C 549/14, Finn Frogne.

of such a contract, it is for the contracting authority not only to use the most appropriate procurement procedures, but also to take care when defining the subject matter of that contract. Furthermore, [...] the contracting authority may retain the possibility of making amendments, even material ones, to the contract, after it has been awarded, on condition that this is provided for in the documents which governed the award procedure. [...] Although the principle of equal treatment and the obligation of transparency must be guaranteed even in regard to specific public contracts, this does not mean that the particular aspects of those contracts cannot be taken into account. That legal imperative and that practical necessity are reconciled, first, through strict compliance with the conditions of a contract as they were laid down in the contract documents up to the end of the implementation phase of that contract, but also, second, through the possibility of making express provision, in those documents, for the option for the contracting authority to adjust certain conditions, even material ones, of that contract after it has been awarded. By expressly providing for that option and setting the rules for the application thereof in those documents, the contracting authority ensures that all economic operators interested in participating in the procurement procedure are aware of that possibility from the outset and are therefore on an equal footing when formulating their respective tenders."

The above-quoted case-law was expressly taken into account in the provisions of the EU Directives on public procurement contracts and concessions, by providing for explicit cases when modifications to contracts may occur without triggering a new award, namely:

- modifications considered non-material, that is, those whose value is below the applicable EU thresholds, and does not reach 10% of the value of the initial contract;
- modifications that, although substantial, do not require a new awarding procedure, provided they comply with specific requirements and do not alter the "general nature" of the contract.

In compliance with the aforementioned principles, however material, some changes do not require a new awarding procedure, that is, those that "irrespective of their monetary value, have been provided for in the initial concession documents in clear, precise and unequivocal review clauses, which may include value revision clauses, or options. Such clauses shall state the scope and nature of possible modifications or options as well as the conditions under which they may be used. They shall not provide for modifications or options that would alter the overall nature of the concession."[3]

However, due to the generally long duration of concession/PPP contracts, as well as the evolution, over time, of the concept of operating risk—whose features have been gradually refined—currently existing concession/PPP contracts may often need re-negotiation in order to preserve their legal nature and balanced allocation of risks. This revision calls for careful execution, since, even when driven by sound economic and financial rationale, nevertheless, such re-negotiations must be assessed from a stringent legal perspective, as any other contract modification. The fundamental criterion is the above-mentioned "material changes." The same applies for the assessment of the risk structure allocated to EOs and the impact of any contractual changes on such allocation. This is because, since concessions/PPPs are long-term contracts, their compliance with the specific nature of the concession type—in particular in relation to the correct allocation of risks—must be verified not only at the time of their signing, but also during their execution, that is, when operational risk materializes. Therefore, where some aspects of a contract, legitimately stipulated according to the regulations in force at the time, become inconsistent with the concession/PPP model emerging from the evolution brought about by case-law, legislation, and practice, a revision of the contract itself is not only allowed, but necessary. Clearly, this review must have the purpose of ensuring the continuing compliance of the contract with the concession/PPP legal model and cannot have the effect of conferring an advantage not initially provided to the concessionaire, nor can it alter the original nature of the contract. Furthermore, it must guarantee compliance with the principles of transparency and equal treatment.

Within this regulatory framework, the revision of the economic and financial plan is, in principle, a contractual amendment too, since such plan is a necessary and fundamental part of the contract itself. In fact, the conditions underpinning the economic and financial plan are the fundamental benchmark for verifying—when awarding the contract—that operating risk is appropriately allocated, while ensuring that the transaction is economically and financially viable and sustainable.

In this context, the provision of a specific contractual clause, precisely defining the conditions and methods for rebalancing the economic and

[3] Article 43 of the EU Directive on concessions.

financial plan in advance, represents a very useful tool, since—to satisfy the public interest in the construction and management of works and delivery of services—the rationale of concession/PPP contracts requires the contract balance to be maintained for the entire duration of the contract. From this point of view, as EOs take on operating risks with the prospect of making a profit, this risk assumption must be based on solid estimates and assumptions, reasonably stable and allowing the allocated risk to be forecasted and monitored. Where such conditions vary—for reasons not attributable to the private partner, especially his inability to fulfil contractual obligations—the appropriate allocation of risks may be jeopardized and contracts can be re-negotiated legitimately. In other words, the provisions on re-negotiation should be triggered whenever the initial balance between the respective obligations allocated between the public and the private party is at risk, for reasons not deriving from poor performance or normal—or, rather, foreseeable—variations in market conditions. Compliance with the principles of equal treatment and transparency, in this context, is therefore ensured by a clear regulation, within the contract, of the conditions triggering re-negotiation, which must be enacted according to the allocation of risks as per the relevant risk matrix. In other words, re-negotiation may only take place if the triggering event is not due to the occurrence of those risks that were transferred to the EO in the first place.

This concept has been implemented in the EU Directive on concessions, whereby "The concessionaire shall be deemed to assume operating risk where, *under normal operating conditions*, it is not guaranteed to recoup the investments made or the costs incurred in operating the works or the services which are the subject-matter of the concession" (emphasis added).

The renegotiation of PPP contracts may imply also a renegotiation of the financial plan, which is analyzed in Chap. 7.

References

Vecchi, V., Casalini, F., & Gatti, S. (2015). Attracting Private Investors: The EU Project Bond Initiative and the Case of A11 Motorway. In S. Caselli, G. Corbetta, & V. Vecchi (Eds.), *Public Private Partnerships for Infrastructure and Business Development*. New York: Palgrave Macmillan.

Vecchi, V., Casalini, F., Cusumano, N., & Leone, V. M. (2020). PPP in Health Care – Trending Toward a Light Model: Evidence From Italy. *Public Works Management and Policy*, *25*(3), 244–258. https://doi.org/10.1177/1087724X20913297.

CHAPTER 5

Project Risks and Optimal Allocation

Veronica Vecchi and Velia M. Leone

Abstract An adequate risk allocation is a distinctive feature of PPP contracts. This chapter illustrates the main risks that could affect a PPP contract, the main rules to secure a correct risks allocation, and how and why to estimate the cost of risks. Risks allocation is also fundamental for the accounting treatment of PPP contracts, especially those based on the payment of the availability fees by the authorities. Therefore, this chapter presents and discusses the sophisticated accounting system for PPP contracts in place in Europe. The chapter also includes a risk matrix (see Appendix), which, per each of the main relevant risks, shows the subject, public or private, that should bear it and the implications of such decision.

Keywords Investment risk • Availability risk • Demand risk • Risks matrix • Accounting rules

5.1 Risks Classification

Chapters 1, 2, and 3 identify adequate risk allocation as a distinctive feature of PPP contracts. Indeed, sound risk allocation is the main advantage of PPP contracts, compared to traditional procurement. Without balanced risk allocation, whereby the appropriate risks are transferred to the private partner, there is no incentive to achieve the expected performance targets in

V. Vecchi et al., *Public Private Partnerships*,
https://doi.org/10.1007/978-3-030-65435-1_5

terms of efficiency (on-time, on-budget) and efficiency/effectiveness (on-quality). Risk allocation is based on two essential elements, namely: a robust and complete set of contract clauses and an accurate design of the payment mechanism, which must be able to incentivize economic operators (EOs) to take on full responsibility for the risks transferred to them, by endeavoring to manage contract performance to minimize the occurrence of such risks, or to mitigate their consequences. If the cost associated with the occurrence of harmful events is higher than the cost needed to avoid it, the EO/special purpose vehicle (SPV) will be likely to implement all possible counter-measures in order to prevent it from happening or to ensure its consequences are mitigated. If input data in the financial plan are fully risk-adjusted, risk allocation is jeopardized because the occurrence of risk would not have a significant impact on the project returns. In other words, the EO/SPV has no incentive to monitor, manage, or mitigate risks. This is especially true in availability-based contracts or in user fee-based PPP with a rigid demand, that is, when revenues are almost fixed.

Appropriate risk allocation is essential to ensure the off-balance sheet treatment of the investment, which is, as mentioned in Chap. 1 and 3, one of the fundamental reasons for choosing PPP rather than traditional procurement. However, the reverse reasoning is more accurate, namely authorities should choose PPP because it ensures better risk allocation, which, in turn, is able to guarantee higher overall quality in contract performance. Once the relevant risks are well allocated, the off-balance sheet treatment is a natural and coherent consequence.

That said, not all risks must be transferred to EOs/SPVs: it is utterly essential that only those risks that can be better managed by EOs/SPVs are borne by them.

Risks in PPP can be classified on the basis of their specific nature: political and regulatory; market or external; technical.

- Political and regulatory risks. These depend on the activities of the State at various levels of governance. They may arise, for example, from planning changes, legal changes, or changes in government policy, that may threaten the interests of project stakeholders. Often, political risk relates to government actions at central or regional levels. In some cases, this type of risk emerges from the behavior of the contracting authority itself. These risks must always be retained by contracting authorities (CAs).
- Macroeconomic and market risks arise from the possibility that the economic environment and the market may change over time.

These risks must be carefully analyzed with reference to the specific context: in some cases, they can be transferred to EOs; in other cases they must be retained by CAs. They require a sophisticated case-by-case evaluation.

- Technical risks are linked to the EO's know-how and the features of the project and technology. They are generally retained by the EOs and include:

- the risk that design/engineering processes fail to perform as expected;
- the risk of faulty building techniques or higher costs in construction;
- the risk that maintenance/service costs are higher than projected; and
- the risk that maintenance/service delivery does not meet the standard required under the contract, but without incurring additional costs.

Table 5.1 shows a possible re-classification of the main project risks belonging to the three categories above, according to project development phases. The table is known as a risk matrix, which is the main tool applied to:

- identify project risks;
- assess their economic significance;
- determine their appropriate allocation; and
- define mitigation strategies and tools.

The most relevant risks that can be transferred to EOs/SPVs are the following: construction (inclusive of design) and availability and/or demand risk. Financial risks may also be critical, especially in emerging economies, where interest and currency rates are very volatile.

Transfer of the construction—or investment—risk happens when all the following elements apply:

- a challenging investment schedule is in place or, at least, no relief measure (for instance, extension of the contract duration) is provided in the event of late completion thereof;
- the contract provides that delays in the delivery of the investment entail a correspondent reduction of the operational phase, thus automatically reducing the volume of revenues and therefore the project return;
- any extra investment cost is intended to be borne by EOs/SPVs.

Table 5.1 Risks classification

Risks	*Political, regulatory, and other risks retained by the CAs*	*Macroeconomic and market risks (the allocation may be on the CA or on the EO/SPV depending on the features of the project and context; these risks can also be shared, wholly or partly)*	*Technical risks transferred to the EO/SPV*	*Comments*
Development phase				
Project coherence with the investment needs	x			If CAs do not carry out an accurate feasibility study before awarding the contract, they may not be able to achieve the desired goals and, therefore, a renegotiation may prove necessary, with potential for higher costs and regulatory issues (at least within the EU legal framework)
Project affordability	x			If the project is too ambitious or some of the risks transferred to the EO are not appropriate, the project may be too expensive for the CA or taxpayers
Quality of the design or the project development			x	If the project is weak, it may result in low-quality construction choices or a longer construction period. This risk is normally transferred by the SPV to project designers and the construction company subcontractor
Longer bidding phase and consequent change of market conditions	x			When the bidding phase is longer than expected, market conditions may have changed in the meanwhile, thereby input data included in the financial plan may prove inadequate. In mature economies, this risk may be (partially) transferred to the SPV

Construction phase					
Project site availability	x	(x)			This risk can be shaped differently, depending on the type of project. It may also be difficult to estimate/manage in the case of network infrastructures, which have extensive needs in terms of land use. As a general rule, the site should be provided by the public sector. In some cases, it might be searched for and purchased by the SPV, which could then be exposed to market risks (volatility in the price) or social risks (i.e. land owners opposing the project development)
Social acceptance	x	(x)			When the SPV retains demand risks, social acceptance risk can influence project profitability; social acceptance can influence the project feasibility, thus generating extra costs for both the CA and the EO. It may also cause reputational damage for the EO and for public manager of the CA
Archaeological risk	x			(x)	In countries with many archaeological sites and associated regulations, this risk should be retained by the CA. Alternatively, the risk could be shared so that the CA bears related costs exceeding a fixed amount
Environment	x				This risk is associated with land pollution. As a general rule, this risk is retained by the CA, as the owner of the project site, unless specific circumstances apply
Technology availability and appropriateness				x	This risk is due to technology obsolescence or inadequacy. It is usually transferred by the SPV to the subcontracting construction company
Reliability of forecasts for construction costs and delivery time				x	This risk is usually transferred by the SPV to the subcontracting construction company

(*continued*)

Table 5.1 (continued)

Risks	*Political, regulatory, and other risks retained by the CAs*	*Macroeconomic and market risks (the allocation may be on the CA or on the EO/SPV depending on the features of the project and context; these risks can also be shared, wholly or partly)*	*Technical risks transferred to the EO/SPV*	*Comments*
Authorizations	x		x	Authorizations depend on the quality of the project/design; in general terms, this risk is borne by the EO/SPV, although the CA is required to cooperate with the SPV to make the process leaner and faster. Some authorizations, however, may be delayed for reasons that are not related to the quality of the design. In such cases, the risk should be retained by the CA or it can be treated as force majeure
Project changes requested by the authority	x			This risk is relevant in countries with political and administrative instability. When project changes imply a different level of funding, this risk may request changes to the financial contract, thereby affecting project bankability

Operating phase					
Change in service tariff, defined by the regulator/authority	X			X	This risk is only relevant for demand-based contracts. It can be retained by the CA or transferred to the EO/SPV, depending on the specific regulatory framework and demand
Volatility of demand		X			This risk is only relevant for demand-based contracts. It can be retained by the CAs or transferred to the EO/SPV, depending on the specific features of the project and context, as discussed in Chap. 3
Underperformance of facilities, causing increases in life cycle or maintenance costs or the need for additional investment				X	This risk is mostly relevant for availability-based contracts. It is usually transferred by the SPV to the subcontracting construction/operating company
The CA does not comply with payment obligations	X				The occurrence of this risk should trigger the payment of interests. However, it can be a serious issue in some emerging countries, especially if the PPP contract absorbs a relevant part of the CA's budget, thus implying the unaffordability of the contract
Changes required by the CA in the level of service	X				When changes are requested by the CA or by the regulator, the associated costs are borne by the CA. However, changes in the level of service may also be needed to match a modified demand: in this case, contract provisions should be accurately drafted in order to clearly identify the acceptable level of variability

(*continued*)

Table 5.1 (continued)

Risks	*Political, regulatory, and other risks retained by the CAs*	*Macroeconomic and market risks (the allocation may be on the CA or on the EO/SPV depending on the features of the project and context; these risks can also be shared, wholly or partly)*	*Technical risks transferred to the EO/SPV*	*Comments*
Underperformance of energy technologies			X	This risk is retained by the SPV and is usually transferred to the subcontracting operating company
Underperformance or faster than expected obsolescence of equipment/technology			X	This risk is especially relevant in availability or supply-based contracts, where it is transferred to the EO/SPV. However, the obsolescence risk can be multifaceted. It can be transferred to the SPV in the case of stable technologies. In the case of particularly long contracts or peculiar technologies that are subject to continuous and/or hardly foreseeable innovation, transferring this risk may prove too expensive
Underperformance or failure of subcontractors		X		This risk is retained by the SPV
Financing				
Availability of affordable financing		X		This risk is retained by the SPV. In some contexts, the CA may be willing to collaborate with the SPV to encourage the participation of development banks in the transaction

Refinancing risk		X		Loans may mature before the end of the contract period, at which point the majority of the loan is still outstanding and the project sponsor will default if the facility is not refinanced. If the result is that interest costs increase, this can increase the portion of cash flow aimed at debt service. This risk is retained by the SPV. In some countries, it may be retained by the CA—e.g. "mini-perm" structures (in which the tenor of the senior debt is shorter than contract duration), which has become more common
Other risks, across the whole life cycle				
Inflation		X		The real value of payments and revenues may be higher or lower than expected at financial close, depending on changes in the relevant price index. As a result, it is typical for payments to be linked to an inflation index (such as the Retail Prices Index—RPI), according to a pre-determined ratio. Hence, both parties bear some degree of inflation risk
Currency exchange rate fluctuation		X		This risk is retained by the SPV and, while it is usually managed through hedging instruments, it can still be a serious issue in some emerging countries
Force majeure		X		Usually, this risk is retained by the CAs or shared
Change in taxation	X			Normally this risk is retained by the CAs
Change in law	X			Normally this risk is retained by the CAs
Stability of business, political, and legal environment	X	X		This risk affects the execution of the contract and the SPV. It may constitute a serious issue in emerging countries, although it can be hedged through guarantees released my multilateral institutions

(*continued*)

Table 5.1 (continued)

Risks	*Political, regulatory, and other risks retained by the CAs*	*Macroeconomic and market risks (the allocation may be on the CA or on the EO/SPV depending on the features of the project and context; these risks can also be shared, wholly or partly)*	*Technical risks transferred to the EO/SPV*	*Comments*
SPV default		X		This risk affects the SPV's equity providers and the CA. Lenders may decide to step in to avoid SPV default and contract termination, in the case of underperformance of the industrial EOs involved in the execution of the contract. CAs may also decide to enter into a contract renegotiation in order to avoid the default of the project, which may cause severe service disruption
Termination value different from expected		X		In general, straight line depreciation is applied and there is no terminal value. Therefore, this risk is generally not significant

Investment risk also includes risk linked to increases in the cost of financing, compared to the forecasts encompassed in the financial plan. This risk is generally mitigated by the SPV by borrowing money at a fixed interest rate or by hedging the cost of the debt. In order to really transfer this risk, it is appropriate to carefully estimate the cost of debt and equity when the financial plan is drafted (more details are included in Chap. 7).

As regards demand risk, it is necessary to carefully assess whether the same is appropriately transferred to OEs/SPVs: if demand is underestimated or is particularly rigid, there is no risk transfer and, therefore, in such cases the option of switching to an availability-based contract may be considered (see Chap. 4 for useful suggestions to achieve an appropriate treatment of the demand risk).

As mentioned in Chap. 4, transfer of availability risk can be quite challenging, as it is heavily influenced by the complexity of the project and the social losses associated with any disruption in the service. For example, in healthcare projects, availability risk is potentially easier to identify because any disruption in the availability of the relevant facility or service can be sanctioned with a deduction/penalty deriving from the social cost generated. Even in these cases, however, assessing the impact of the deductions/penalties on the financial plan is of the utmost importance in order to achieve an adequate balance. If the deductions/penalties provided are set at an excessive level, they could discourage EOs and make the contract too expensive because forecasted costs to mitigate the specific risk would be too high. By contrast, high deductions/penalties could be used when non-availability risk is fairly low, for example, for low-complexity investments such as schools.

In any event, in order to maintain the appropriate risk allocation—as agreed, at the outset, by the contract—contract renegotiation can only be allowed in the event that a change in those risks retained by CAs occurred. In general, these risks belong to the political and regulatory realm, as described above, and they are:

- modifications to some of the project elements (during the construction or the management phase) requested by the CA due to modified needs, provided they do not change the essential features or the nature of the contract;
- force majeure, although it is important to promote full collaboration by the SPVs in case some force majeure events should occur—such as with the provision of a "grace period" between the event and the possibility to request renegotiation;

- delays in the release of authorizations by the CA or in the availability of the relevant site;
- delays or higher costs due to non-acceptance of the contract/project by the community, that is the so-called social acceptance;
- higher taxation, though the relevant consequences should trigger renegotiation only when they affect project returns in a significant way (for instance, when their impact is above a certain pre-determined range of return variability);
- changes in law.

Such events may generate not only higher costs for EOs/SPVs, but also lower costs; in the latter case, renegotiation should be in favor of the CAs.

5.2 Estimating the Cost of Risks

In order to accurately estimate the cost of a risk (the so-called expected cost), the following formula should be applied:

$$\rho_1 \times \text{cost}_1 + \rho_2 \times \text{cost}_2 + \rho_3 \times \text{cost}_3$$

Where:
the sum of probabilities $\rho_{1 \ldots} \rho_n$ makes 1
Cost_{1-n} is the cost associated to each probability.

However, as mentioned, this methodology would significantly reduce the risk exposure of EOs/SPVs if it is used on an ex ante basis, that is, in order to define the costs to be included in the financial plan. This method is useful for understanding the actual relevance of each risk. Indeed, the CAs' tendency may be to underestimate the impact of risks and, for private investors, to overestimate it.

The above methodology can also be applied by CAs to define an appropriate system of deductions/penalties and, therefore, to set them at an appropriate level. Indeed, since the probability of certain risks actually occurring is fairly low, without such a rigorous approach, CAs may intentify and quantify deductions/penalties utterly ineffective. That said, it should be remembered that project risks are multiple, and the appropriate risk allocation requires a comprehensive approach, to be designed on the basis of the specific features of each individual project and the corresponding jurisdiction.

Box 5.1 provides an example to understand how to calculate the overall risk borne by EOs/SPVs.

Box 5.1 How to calculate the overall risk borne by EOs/SPVs in PPP contracts

To calculate the overall risk borne by EOs/SPVs, it is important to prepare an accurate risk matrix and to quantify the cost associated with the risks transferred, with reference to those more likely to occur.

For the sake of our example, we can consider the following risks as the most probable:

1. Construction risk
2. Demand risk
3. Supply/availability risk, deriving from changes in the operational costs due to a lower service or technology performance, changes in the demand or new solutions that may increase the efficiency but imply higher costs
4. Inflation risks, since payment by the authority are fixed, without any inflation-indexation.

The overall expected cost of such risks, calculated on the basis of their probabilities of occurring, is set, in the example, at €1,986,495.

In the most negative scenario (*worst case*), that is, in the event that all of the above risks should happen and with the greatest impact (meaning an increase in the construction costs by 15%, a one-year extension of the construction period, reduced revenues by 2%, an increase in operating costs by 10%, and an increase in the inflation rate up to 2% per year), the overall loss is estimated at €4,686,536.

Risk of increase in the construction cost	Increase in construction costs compared to the value included in the financial plan	Probability of occurring	Loss (impact on the net present value in €)
	0%	40%	0
	5%	35%	-34,999
	10%	15%	-70,243
	15%	10%	-105,609
	Expected value of the risk		**-38,609**

(*continued*)

Box 5.1 (continued)

Risk of extension of construction period	Increase in the length of the construction phase	Probability of occurring	Loss (impact on the net present value in €)
	0	30%	0
	6 months	40%	-80,819
	1 year	30%	-127,905
	Expected value of the risk		**-70,699**
Demand risk (risk of a reduced demand/ revenue volume)	Changes in the demand	Probability of occurring	Loss (impact on the net present value in €)
	-2%	10%	-429,100
	-1%	40%	-211,620
	0%	25%	0
	1%	20%	210,553
	2%	5%	420,350
	Expected value of the risk		**-64,430**
Availability risk (increase in operating costs needed to match demand)	Increase in operating costs	Probability of occurring	Loss (impact on the net present value in €)
	-10%	10%	1,735,905
	-5%	10%	870,513
	0%	30%	0
	5%	30%	-1,825,478
	10%	20%	-890,531
	Expected value of the risk		**-465,108**
Inflation risk	Changes in the inflation rate	Probability of occurring	Loss (impact on the net present value in €)
	0%	40%	0
	1%	30%	-1358.773
	2%	30%	-3,133,391
	Expected value of the risk		**-1,347,649**
	Overall expected value of risks (€)		**-1,986,495**
	worst case scenario (€)		**-4,686,536**

5.3 PPP Accounting in the European Union

Eurostat, the statistical office of the European Union, which dictates the rules for the calculation of debt and deficit of all Member States, has a dedicated chapter, in the Manual on Government Debt and Deficit (Eurostat 2016), on the accounting treatments of PPP contracts. This clarifies that a PPP contract—according to Eurostat, a contract where the public authority is the main payer[1]—can be accounted for off-balance sheet, without associating a debt liability to the new investment amount. This is only the case if risks are demonstrably transferred to the private sector such that there is a meaningful threat to private investors' profitability (thus creating a strong incentive to manage or neutralize risks). In particular, there are three relevant general categories of risk for Eurostat: construction, demand, and availability. At least two of these must be allocated to the EO/SPV to treat the contract off-balance sheet.

These risks are defined as follows by Eurostat in the 2016 Edition (pag. 340):

- Construction risk covers events related to possible difficulties faced during the construction phase and to the state of the involved asset(s) at the time when the services start to be provided. In practice, it is related to events such as late delivery, non-respect of specified standards, significant additional costs, legal and environmental issues, technical deficiency, and external negative effects (including environmental risk) triggering compensation payments to third parties.
- Availability risk covers cases where, during the operation of the asset, the responsibility of the partner is called upon, because of faulty management ("bad performance"), resulting in a volume of services lower than that contractually agreed upon, or in services not meeting the specified quality standards.

[1]According to Eurostat the term PPPs "will be exclusively used to describe those long-term contracts in which government pays to a non-government partner all or a majority of the fees under a specific contractual arrangement, thus covering most of the total cost of the service provided (including the amortisation of the assets). In national accounts, this feature distinguishes PPPs from concessions. In a concession contract, government makes no regular payments to the partner, or such payments, if they exist, do not constitute a majority of fees received by the partner. In a PPP contract, the final users do not pay directly (i.e. in a way proportional to the use of the asset and clearly identified only for this use), or only for a minor part (and generally for some specific uses of the asset), for the use of the assets for which a service will be provided".

- Demand risk covers the variability of demand (higher or lower than expected at the time when the contract was signed), irrespective of the performance of the partner. In other words, a shift of demand cannot be directly and totally linked to an insufficient quality of the services provided by the partner, although quantitative and qualitative shortfalls in this matter are likely to have an impact on the effective use of the service and, in some cases, exert an eviction effect. Instead, the demand risk may also result from other factors, such as the business cycle, new market trends, a change in final users' preferences, or technological obsolescence. This must be seen as part of the usual "economic risk" borne by EOs in a market economy.

The demand risk can also be assumed by the EO when the payment is carried out by the CA. In this case, the authority pays on the basis of the use of the facilities; however, in general, the demand is pretty rigid. Further, according to Eurostat, off-balance sheet treatment is possible when the grant or debt guarantee awarded by the CA to the SPV is less than 50% of the capital value of the project. In case of riskier financial tools being used by the CA to support the project, such as junior or subordinated debt, the amount invested must be multiplied by a factor of 2.5 to assess compliance with the 50% threshold. This means that, in the case of subordinated debt invested in the project by the public authority, a maximum amount of 20% is allowed to keep the investment off-balance sheet.

In the context of the European Union, risk allocation is, therefore, salient to ensure the off-balance sheet accounting of PPP contracts, especially for those based on the payment of the availability fee.

Appendix

The risk matrix shown in Table 5.1 is intentionally broad, in order to be applicable across sectors. However, some risks may not be relevant in all cases or may be identified differently, according to the specific features of each contract. Each contract has its peculiarities: therefore, it is fundamental to draft the contract and risk allocation on the basis of the specific context and the expected results. Risks are listed according to the project phase in which they may occur, and their allocation depends on the category in which they fall, as discussed above.

The above risk matrix is a useful tool to understand the nature and allocation of the main risks to the contractual parties. In practice, the risk

Table 5.2 Information to be included in the risk matrix

Risk description	*Each risk should be described with specific reference to the features of the specific project*
Relevance of the risks	Since each project is different, the impact of each risk may also change from one project to another. It is, therefore, important to understand its specific relevance in the context of the individual project execution. Relevance may be expressed in a qualitative way (e.g. very high, high, medium, low, very low, or not relevant) or in a quantitative way, through a probability (ρ) or a probability range. Probability ranges can be: not relevant (ρ = 0%–4%), very low (ρ = 5%–15%), low (ρ = 16%–30%), medium (ρ = 31%–50%), high (ρ = 51%–70%), very high (ρ > 71%)
Risk allocation	This element shows whether the risk is retained by the CA or is transferred to EO/SPV
Reference to the contract	Since risk allocation is regulated by the PPP contract, it can be useful to also include a reference to the relevant contract clauses or to its annexes, i.e. where the treatment of the specific risk is regulated
Economic value of the risk	This element shows the economic quantification of the risk or, in financial terms, the impact that it may have on the project. The economic value may be different depending on whether the same risk is managed by the CA or by the SPV or any of its subcontractors. Actually, the EO know-how can reduce the likely impact of the risk and its consequences for the project
Risks mitigation strategies and tools	Especially for private investors, it is useful to understand the mitigation strategies and tools that EOs/SPVs may be able to put in place to limit the impact of each risk. Therefore, only risks retained by the SPV and not transferred to subcontractors or hedged—through insurance or other financial products—may benefit from a risk premium to be included in the calculation of the expected return on the equity invested (see Chap. 7)

matrix should be structured in a more detailed way in order to support all necessary evaluation tasks. As it is a tool to support the evaluation of the public and private counterparts together. It is important that it is structured and used in a flexible way. Table 5.2 summarizes some further information that needs to be included in a well-balanced risk matrix.

CHAPTER 6

From Traditional to Outcome-based Public-Private Partnerships: Social Impact Bonds

Francesca Casalini and Veronica Vecchi

Abstract Social impact bonds (SIBs) have emerged in recent years as outcome-based public-private partnerships (PPP) for the delivery of welfare services, whereby economic operators' remuneration is based on their capacity to achieve service outcomes, thus improving contracting authorities' ability to tackle specific social needs. Despite the different nuances, this chapter discusses whether SIBs can be regarded as a first step to testing the feasibility of linking the investors' payment to outcomes and, therefore, as a scheme that could be extended to traditional infrastructure-based PPP contracts.

Keywords Social impact bonds • Outcome-based contracts • Social impact • Measurability • Social innovation

6.1 The Rise of SIBs

Using public-private partnerships (PPP) as a policy tool to achieve better effectiveness in the delivery of public services, especially the social ones, requires changing the contract model. Moving from traditional PPP

V. Vecchi et al., *Public Private Partnerships*,
https://doi.org/10.1007/978-3-030-65435-1_6

models—mainly focused on efficiency—contracting authorities (CAs) should switch toward outcome-based PPP, whereby economic operators' (EOs) remuneration is based on their capacity to achieve service outcomes, thus improving CAs' ability to tackle specific social needs.

This new approach should be welcomed by that part of the private sector which, in recent years, has been increasingly incorporating societal and environment aspects into its investment decisions, as discussed in Chap. 1.

Among the different forms of social investing, social impact bonds (SIBs) can be defined as public-private plural partnerships, according to Henry Minztberg (2015), with a contractual structure very similar to the availability-based PPP model (i.e. aimed at financing and delivering welfare services). SIBs, indeed, were conceived not only to overcome the typical shortcomings of traditional public and third-sector service provision (i.e. lack of capital, need for performance management, low efficiency, and accountability), but also to bring more innovation to service design and delivery in order to encourage key stakeholders to focus on the achievement of higher social outcomes.

SIBs are an innovative contractual and financing mechanism in which authorities enter into agreements with social service providers, such as social enterprises or non-profit organizations, and private investors to pay for the delivery of predefined social outcomes. SIBs—whose name was first conceived in the UK—are also known as outcome-based contracts (Continental Europe), pay-for-success contracts (US) or pay-for-benefits contracts (Australia). After the first SIB project was launched in the UK in 2010, more than 130 projects, for a total of €370 million, have been implemented at international level to date and more than 70 are in the development phase.[1] Although SIBs were mainly applied in developed countries, they have also been experimented within developing countries, in the form of development impact bonds (DIBs).

In essence, SIBs involve a set of contracts based on a CA's decision to pay for an improvement with a specific social outcome, but only once it has been achieved by the EO. Authorities can decide to award SIBs in order to improve a particular social outcome or to tackle unmet needs in the social field. Investors provide the upfront capital to deliver the intervention, thus assuming the financial risk. These funds are passed on to service providers, generally through an intermediary, to cover investment

[1] Source: Social Finance, as in September 2020. https://www.socialfinance.org.uk.

and/or operating costs needed for the delivery of specific actions intended for a selected target group of beneficiaries. If the measurable outcomes agreed upon at the outset are achieved, the CA will repay the investors for their initial investment, plus a return for the financial risks they took. In the case of lower or higher performance in the achievement of the target outcomes, the payment will be, respectively, higher or lower; in the latter case, no payment is due if no outcome is generated. In other words, if the EO is not able to generate the expected outcomes, payment from the CA is reduced, or cancelled, and no return on the investment is generated. With regards to this financial structure, in spite of their name, SIBs cannot be regarded as bonds in the conventional sense since the capital invested is similar to a riskier equity investment, generally provided by one or few investors.

Given the set of contracts involved, the upfront capital provided by private investors and the payment made by the CA (provided predetermined performance standards are met) SIBs have been regarded as an expansion of the long-term infrastructure PPP model into social program delivery. However, the focus of this form of partnership is no longer an infrastructure-based service, as in traditional PPP schemes, but social issues that require new approaches to be tackled. Indeed, the SIB model fosters not only efficiency—in terms of on-time, on-budget, and on-quality delivery—but also effectiveness, in terms of actual impact and value generated for society. In other words, SIBs encourage social innovation, which occurs at the intersection of the public, private, and social sectors.

A classic SIB scheme involved a plurality of stakeholders, as shown in Fig. 6.1. On the one hand, we have the private sector—encompassing both private investors (providing upfront capital) and non-profit service providers (bringing unique expertise in innovative service delivery approaches). On the other hand, we have the public sector—which sets the social goals and has the capacity to develop an overarching coordination framework. An independent evaluator usually measures the impact of the project according to predetermined outcome metrics. Co-production with service users, families, and voluntary carers is also encouraged. For these reasons, the SIB model can bring about the paradigmatic shift from New Public Management toward New Public Governance and Public Value, whereby the creation of public value founds its practice on dialogue, exchange, and co-creation among relevant interest groups. The fundamental underpinning mechanism of SIBs relies upon the measurement of social outcomes and the generation of cashable savings as a result

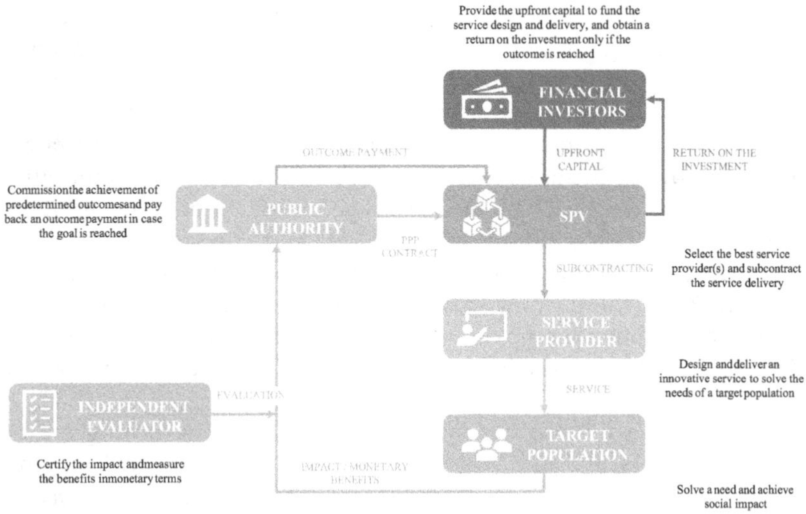

Fig. 6.1 The SIB Scheme. (Source: Authors)

of improved outcomes (e.g. lower recidivism rates will accrue savings in police, courts, prison, probation, etc.). Ideally, the savings in public service budgets are used to fund the repayment of the intervention plus the financial return to private investors. Experiences, such as the Rikers Island SIB (see Box 6.1), demonstrate that, regardless, the fundamental condition to pay the private counterpart is the achievement of the social outcomes. This mechanism has been regarded as a way to improve performance management and measurement in social service delivery, introduce greater efficiency and accountability for authorities and service providers, and increase innovation and personalization of services. However, this mechanism has raised some concerns on the viability of SIBs. On one hand, establishing a direct causal link between an intervention and its outcome is generally complex but, on the other hand, cashable savings may be difficult to estimate at the outset as they are usually achieved in the long term and results may not be clearly attributable to one single authority's budget. However, what is appreciable is the will of private investors to take the risk of making their return conditional upon a third party's ability to reach social outcomes.

Public-private-plural partnerships such as SIBs—as per Henry Minzberg's definition—could represent the right vehicle both to capture the increasing social awareness of private investors and to support the public sector to achieve higher effectiveness and equity in its action, together with increased efficiency and accountability.

6.2 SIBs' Features Emerging from International Experiences

After the first SIB was launched in 2010, the number of deals has grown consistently, with the majority of projects concentrated in the past few years. Such initiatives were mainly developed in Europe and North America. The highest number of SIBs is found in the UK, where their implementation has been policy-driven (top-down approach). Leveraging the money coming from the Big Lottery Fund, the government set up seven investment funds with a total of £191 million in funding,[2] which commissioning authorities can use—upon application—for SIB outcome payments. SIBs are also used in the US, Australia, and Canada, as well as in continental European countries such as Portugal and the Netherlands. In the latter countries, SIBs have been mainly developed through a bottom-up approach, that is, promoted by private partners (mainly philanthropic investors such as foundations and charities).

In Europe, SIBs have been used to tackle social problems in the area of workforce development, particularly focusing on youth and refugee unemployment, and homelessness, with projects mainly focusing on housing as well as support provision to vulnerable people. By contrast, in the US, they have been applied in the area of criminal justice, to reduce prisoners' recidivism. In some cases, the services conceived within the SIBs can be considered innovative (i.e. programs based on a new configuration, approach, therapy, etc.), while in other cases, they are based on an expansion of existing practices (i.e. programs already tested scaled up and applied to other target beneficiaries). The unmet social issues that SIBs have addressed so far were either already covered by existing, though ineffective, public services, or uncovered. In the former case, the CA has a budget that can be used to pay the investors and a baseline of current costs to estimate potential savings. In the latter case, no budget is available and, therefore, extra resources have to be budgeted in to cover SIB outcome payments.

[2] https://www.gov.uk/guidance/social-impact-bonds.

So far, SIBs have an average duration of up to four or five years. This rather short length is due to the small size of the upfront investment. Actually, the financial value of implemented SIBs has been, on average, €3 million, but 50% of projects have a budget of less than €1.5 million. This confirms that SIBs are low capital-intensive—as they focus on service, instead of infrastructure provision—and so far, they have been mainly applied on small-scale initiatives.

In terms of financial structure, despite the name and as previously explained, SIBs are not bond-like instruments, but they have been mainly funded through private debt and equity. The type of security used and, in many cases, the issue of a guarantee (provided either by public authorities or private philanthropic investors) have significantly affected the risk profile of SIBs. The UK-based SIBs have been generally structured as equity investments since they are based on ad hoc funds, while in the US and Continental Europe, debt-like structures secured through a guarantee are more common. The drawdown of the upfront capital and the payment of the outcome fee have followed different structures and schedules, according to the timing of the activities and the outcome measurement,[3] thereby affecting also the return earned by private investors.

The return profile has been quite variable and, in many cases, undisclosed. In case the social outcome is achieved, the outcome payment has been set, on average, at 190% compared to the initial investment, within a range that goes from 100% (i.e. just capital reimbursement) to 500% (i.e. a payment five times greater than the investment). In case of underperformance, in some projects the payment has been reduced to zero, while, in other projects, a guarantee was provided, in order to cover up to 95% of the initial investment. Furthermore, in terms of IRR, implemented SIBs have targeted, on average, a 5.20% on an annual basis, within a range that goes from 1% to 12%. In most cases, if the social outcome achieved is above the target, the actual IRR is higher than the target IRR, but a maximum IRR (i.e. a cap) is defined.

[3] If the service is delivered to more than one cohort of beneficiaries over a period of more than one year, payments have been usually made in multiple tranches. If no intermediate output is set and it is expected that results are achieved and measured at the end, or even after the end, of the intervention, the repayment has been made in one single tranche at the maturity.

SIB contracts involve, as a rule, the following categories of investors:

1. Foundations, charitable organizations, and religious institutions: they represent the majority of SIB investors.
2. Impact investors: impact investing firms are specialized asset managers with the mandate to commit capital to enterprises and projects that pursue both social and financial returns. They represent the second largest group of investors in SIBs.
3. Mainstream investors: banks and traditional financial intermediaries are only involved in a few SIB projects. They commit money within their CSR policies or, when protected by guarantees, within their standard asset management portfolios; the latter case is often a way to provide alternative investment opportunities to their high net worth individual investors.

In the majority of cases, foundations and impact investing firms have acted as hands-on investors, meaning that they have played as originator of the SIB as well as anchor investor (i.e. they have conceived and designed the project and looked for other investors). Impact investing firms are a perfect fit for SIBs. In the majority of cases, these investors manage dedicated SIB funds, which are invested on a commercial basis with clear target financial IRR. Foundations, given their concerted focus on addressing key social challenges and their willingness to invest on a non-repayable basis, have not invested in SIB on a commercial basis; in some cases, they have not only provided the funding to cover part of the cost of the intervention, but also provided a guarantee to reduce other investors' capital losses. When guarantees are provided by philanthropic organizations, as in the case of the Rikers Island SIB (see Box 6.1), they have stimulated mainstream investors to experiment with SIB investments, which otherwise would not have been possible given the lower risk appetite of this type of investor. Other relevant constraints, such as SIB small average deals' size and the difficult fit of SIBs within their usual asset allocation framework, prevent many mainstream investors from allocating capital to these instruments.

So far, investors in SIBs have been mainly foundations, motivated by testing out the instrument rather than setting optimal contractual and financial incentives. As a consequence, as discussed above, the return profile of SIBs is quite variable and there is no evidence on how these returns have been calculated. In many cases, foundations have acted as intermediary organizations, facilitating the selection of the most appropriate, efficient, and effective service provider. In other cases, the intermediary has been a specialized organization or an SPV (i.e. special purpose vehicle, a specific legal entity created ad hoc to implement the project). In some cases, service providers were the SPV's shareholders, even though, in most cases, they have generally acted as mere sub-contractors.

Although so far, SIBs developed across the world show certain common elements (i.e. payment conditional on target outcomes, impact measurement, involvement of a plurality of public and private stakeholders), at the same time, there is considerable variety in the way these initiatives have been initiated and structured. This is clearly evidenced when considering, for example, project's promoters, level of innovation of the intervention, financial structure and return, type of investor involved. Box 6.1 highlights the differences between two cases of implemented SIBs.

6.3 Some Critical Reflections on SIBs

The main rationale for introducing SIBs is the need to improve outcome delivery through innovation in the provision of social services provision. However, international experiences show that the majority of SIBs are based on already implemented and well-established models delivered by service providers with proven track records (Vecchi and Casalini 2019). One possible explanation for this trend could be that investors motivated by a return on investment have little incentive to fund risky innovative experiments. Some argue that SIBs merely represent the continuation of the effort of successive UK governments to reduce direct public intervention in social services whilst simultaneously encouraging increased investment from the private sector and marketing for the third sector. Since social innovation is risky, it should imply a strategic role of the government, even through forms of financial support or risk sharing, which is exactly the opposite of a SIB model that is based on a complete risks' transfer to the private sector. Actually, evidence from past international SIBs shows that, in many cases, private investors do not bear the risk of achieving the social outcomes since commissioning public authorities or, more frequently, philanthropic investors (such as foundations) provide guarantees to cover up to 95% of capital losses. Despite the risk of adverse selection and moral hazard when guarantees are used (as discussed in Chap. 2), well-designed guarantees may be important to mitigate the risks associated with innovative experiments and sustain the attraction of private capital into SIBs, especially in their early phases of development.

Box 6.1 A comparison of two SIB experiences

In this box, two cases of SIBs are discussed. The first was implemented in Birmingham (UK) in the sector of youth homelessness and unemployment, the second on Rikers Island (NY, US), in the field of criminal justice. The Birmingham SIB follows the UK standard model; it was commissioned following a top-down approach, the scope of the intervention can be regarded as innovative and the financial structure consists of an unsecured equity investment. By contrast, the Rikers Island SIB is an example of a bottom-up approach, consisting in the expansion of existing interventions and presenting a debt-like financial structure secured through a guarantee provided by a philanthropic investor. While the Birmingham SIB was funded by Bridges Ventures, the largest impact investing firm worldwide, the Rikers Island SIB received money from Goldman Sachs, one of the biggest American investment banks.

Birmingham SIB[4]

This SIB was commissioned by the UK Department for Communities and Local Government (DCLG) and the Cabinet Office as part of the Fair Chance Fund. Focused on Birmingham, Coventry, Walsall, and Solihull, its aim was to support around 300 of the most vulnerable young people into accommodation, education, training, and employment. Social Finance acted as the intermediary company, while the non-profit organization, St. Basils, delivered the service. A pool of impact investors provided the upfront capital to cover the cost of the intervention. This SIB reached its end on 31 December 2017. Outcomes were particularly strong compared to targets, with 102 young people entering full- or part-time employment against a target of 75, and 290 young people entering stable accommodation, against a target of 250.

Program: The Rewriting Futures program supported 300 young people aged 18–24. The program consisted in providing a housing solution as well as innovative personal coaching, thereby featuring a relevant and supportive link into education, employment, and the community.

Target outcomes: Out of the 300 young people targeted, the program aimed to support at least 250 into accommodation, 200 into education, and 75 into sustained employment. Measurement of results was made quarterly.

Financial structure: Bridges Ventures, Big Issue Invest, CAF Venturesome, Barrow Cadbury Trust, and The Key Fund provided £1 million equity to fund the intervention. In the event of success, the maximum aggregate payment made by the DCLG to investors would have been £2.5 million.

[4] Sources: http://www.bridgesfundmanagement.com/portfolio/st-basils/, https://www.socialfinance.org.uk/projects/fair-chance-fund—-st-basils, https://www.gov.uk/government/news/23-million-to-help-homeless-turn-around-their-lives.

(*continued*)

Box 6.1 (continued)

Rikers Island SIB[5]
The project launched in 2012 to support the delivery of therapeutic services to 16- to 18-year-olds incarcerated on Rikers Island was the first SIB implemented in the US. It represented a partnership between the City of New York (commissioning authority), the Department of Correction (paying authority), Bloomberg Philanthropies (the foundation promoting the project, which provided a guarantee to reduce the risk borne by private investors), Goldman Sachs (private investor), MDRC (intermediary), the Osborne Association, and Friends of Island Academy (non-profit service providers). In 2015, the Vera Institute of Justice (independent evaluator) concluded that the intervention had failed to reduce the recidivism rate as targeted. The initiative was, therefore, discontinued and no payments were made to Goldman Sachs, thus triggering the guarantee provided by Bloomberg Philanthropies.
Program: The Adolescent Behavioral Learning Experience (ABLE) program involved 4458 young men aged 16–18 entering the NYC jail on Rikers Island and at risk of reoffending. The ABLE program was designed following the Moral Reconation Therapy, developed in 1985 and widely used in prisons, jails, residential juvenile facilities, drug courts, probation programs, and schools.
Target outcomes: Recidivism rate within the treated group of people was expected to fall at least by 10% compared to the historical group. This would have generated a maximum of $20 million long-term savings for the City of New York.
Financial structure: Goldman Sachs provided a $9.6 million loan to fund the intervention. Bloomberg Philanthropies guaranteed $7.2 million of this investment. In the event of success, the payment made by the Department of Correction to Goldman Sachs would have been $11.7 million, equal to a 5.1% IRR.

Another key rationale behind SIBs is that, within incentive-based contracts, private stakeholders would be able to generate higher social outcomes than the public sector alone. This would result in reduced costs for the public sector and increased value for society. The underpinning mechanism of SIBs relies upon the realization of savings for the public sector, as a result of improved outcomes, which ultimately would be used to deliver a higher financial return to private investors. International experiences show that a value for money (VfM) analysis has usually been carried out in order to assess the desirability of a SIB and to quantify the expected savings for the CA. While traditional VfM applied to PPP typically focuses solely on the financial costs (risk-adjusted) of the different investment

[5] Sources: www.nyc.gov/html/om/pdf/2012/sib_fact_sheet.pdf, https://www.frbsf.org/community-development/files/rikers-island-first-social-impact-bond-united-states.pdf.

options (see Chap. 8), VfM methodology, when applied to SIBs, represents a first attempt to go beyond the mere financial value and quantify, in monetary terms, the impact of improved outcomes. However, it must be noticed that, so far, the focus has been much more on the realization of savings in the public budget as a result of improved outcomes, rather than on the improved outcomes themselves (e.g. savings in police, courts, prison, probation, etc., due to lower recidivism rates, rather than the value of lower recidivism rates for society). This approach could induce governments and service providers to prefer more standard programs, which may generate short-term savings but have limited long-term social impact. The short-term perspective may also be preferred by investors because results are easier to quantify, and the risk of default is lower.

6.4 Can SIBs' Experience and Philosophy be Applied to Traditional PPP Contracts?

Despite the different nuances, SIBs could be regarded as a first step to testing the feasibility of linking the investors' payment to social outcomes and, therefore, as a scheme that could be extended back to infrastructure-based PPP contracts, in a sort of virtual circle reasoning, since we have argued that SIBs originated from PPPs. This calls into question whether a "SIB-like" PPP could be an appropriate solution to attract more private investors able to provide financial resources in order to close the infrastructure gap by focusing on projects that maximize public value.

Past international SIBs show that, although they have been developed in a "protected" environment, thanks to the commitment and financial support of philanthropic organizations, the model has been generally applied to small-scale projects, at local level, with limited risk transfer to financial investors and little innovative scope. Drawing on this evidence, we may deduce that the amount of money requested to develop hard infrastructure, the long-term perspective to generate social results, the risk-adverse profile of long-term investors generally involved in such projects, and their preference for standardized solutions could make the application of the SIB model to infrastructure-based PPP harder. Furthermore, to make the SIB model applicable to infrastructure projects—especially in the social field—and to reach more challenging social outcomes, EOs should be involved in the delivery of core services. However, this is not always possible because such services usually remain the exclusive responsibility of the public sector, at least in mature economies. Moreover, while a social outcome can only be reached through a service (which cannot be limited to building and adequately maintaining a facility), it is clear that linking financial return to social outcomes (which is the essence of SIBs) without involving the private partner in the delivery of the service would be impossible. Since PPP has generated a lot of criticism among politicians and public opinion, especially in mature economies, it may be difficult to extend the experiment of the SIB model to social infrastructure if one of the prerequisites thereof is the extension of the contract scope to core services. Perhaps small-scale PPP initiatives, in specialized sectors such as that of medical equipment, could draw some features from the SIB experience. In fact, it has been observed that some industrial investors may be willing to accept being paid on the basis of the health-value achieved (Porter 2009). In emerging countries, SIBs could be suitable for the implementation of more complex infrastructure investments, also in the framework of blended finance mechanisms offered by supranational organizations. The social challenges raised by Covid-19 pandemic will certainly spur new needs, which public authorities may be able to satisfy through engaging in social innovation and new approaches to public-private collaboration. Box 6.2 includes some considerations, under a legal perspective, on how to extend SIB rationale to PPP contracts, to generate a new form of outcome-based PPPs.

Box 6.2 SIB-like PPPs from a legal perspective[6]

The distinctive feature of SIBs—or outcome-based contracts—is the assumption of risks linked to the outcome of the project involved. This additional risk could be qualified as a more advanced form of the operating risk, which needs to be transferred in concession/PPP models (as explained in Chap. 3). From a legal point of view, therefore, SIBs could be included within the open category of PPP contracts. However, outcome risk goes beyond what is generally accepted by private partners in PPPs as a typical contract obligation, based on the achievement of the agreed level of performance. Moreover, in classic SIB models, such risk is not borne directly by EOs performing the contract (receiving the agreed payment for the services rendered), but is borne by the investor, who, paradoxically, is not involved in any direct contract activity.

Therefore, although, it is conceivable for SIB models to be applied to PPP contracts, it is, however, necessary to carefully adapt the classical SIB schemes. First of all, the sectors in which they can be applied

[6] The box is written by Velia M. Leone.

(*continued*)

Box 6.2 (continued)

must be adequately selected. Social services—also known as "services of general interest" within the meaning of the EU legal framework—can either have an economic nature (SGEI) or be based on pure solidarity principles, therefore, being fully paid by the public sector through general taxation (SGI). SGIs do not allow for the transfer of operating risk. In fact, where SGIs are outsourced, they are usually entrusted to non-profit operators through traditional procurement contracts. An accurate choice of the sector involved is therefore fundamental in order to avoid entering into invalid contracts.

Moreover, PPP contracts cannot be based on unrealistic or poorly constructed outcomes that cannot reasonably be forecasted with a sufficient level of accuracy and, therefore, cannot be factored into the economic and financial planning of any EO. Economic and financial balance is a pre-requisite for entering into a PPP contract. However, in highly regulated sectors or areas, for instance, in the public healthcare sector, the expected outcomes may be determined by a series of factors beyond the competence and reach of the service provider. Therefore, in such cases it is not appropriate to transfer an outcome risk that the EO cannot estimate, nor manage.

Furthermore, engaging in SIB-like PPPs requires a very careful identification of both the scope of contract—in terms of output—and the value outcome to reach. The latter could be set in terms of savings or invariance of public expenditure, or, more realistically, of concrete advantages (quantifiable according to clear and objective criteria) for service users or targets. In a view to designing an appropriate risk balance, it is necessary to identify a system of indicators and parameters suitable for detecting the actual achievement of the expected results and, at the same time, appropriately monitoring their progress, during contract execution.

In practice, in order to apply SIB-like models to PPP contracts, the remuneration system should be adjusted, so as to provide for a first level of payment, linked to performance (in the classic PPP sense) and a second level of payment, conditional upon achieving the desired outcome. In this way, traditional operating risk would apply to PPPs' typical—or even challenging—output requirements, while reaching further outcomes would trigger additional rewards. This methodology necessarily internalizes a certain flexibility, during the execution of the contract, further incentivizing EOs. Such flexibility is allowed, under EU legal frameworks, provided it is appropriately regulated within the contract from the outset (see Chap. 3 for further reference on contract flexibility clauses).

References

Mintzberg, H. (2015). *Time for the Plural Sector.* Stanford Social Innovation Review, Summer 2015.

Porter, M. E. (2009). A Strategy for Health Care Reform—Toward a Value-Based System. *New England Journal of Medicine, 361*(2), 109–112.

Vecchi, V., & Casalini, F. (2019). Is a Social Empowerment of PPP for Infrastructure Delivery Possible? Lessons from Social Impact Bonds. *Annals of Public and Cooperative Economics, 90*(2), 353–369.

CHAPTER 7

Principles of Capital Budgeting for Infrastructure Financing

Francesca Casalini and Veronica Vecchi

Abstract Many of the drawbacks of existing public-private partnership (PPP) projects can be explained by weak financial analyses. This chapter discusses how to apply capital budgeting tools to infrastructure financing, providing guidance principles for public managers, investors, and financial analysts. It claims that when both the contracting authority and the private counterparts develop sound financial analyses for the project, they are able to better craft the PPP contract and reduce the extent of information asymmetry during the procurement and implementation phases.

Keywords Financial plan • Capital budgeting • Economic and financial equilibrium • Cost of capital • Renegotiation of financial conditions

7.1 The Aim of Capital Budgeting for Infrastructure Financing

Capital budgeting, or investment appraisal, is the planning process used to determine whether a long-term investment is worth the deployment of cash through the capitalization structure (debt and equity).

V. Vecchi et al., *Public Private Partnerships*,
https://doi.org/10.1007/978-3-030-65435-1_7

Traditional capital budgeting/finance textbooks focus their attention on private investments. With some caveat, capital budgeting principles are applied to public-private partnership (PPP) contracts, and more in general to the appraisal of infrastructures and services, to drive decisions in the public and private sectors.

As shown in Fig. 7.1, capital budgeting analyses serve multiple purposes. From a public sector perspective, capital budgeting is fundamental to assessing the most feasible and appropriate investment among a range of options (e.g. to compare a "do minimum" option—i.e. renovation of an existing facility—with a "do maximum" option—i.e. brand-new construction). Further, it is applied to analyze the value for money of different options (i.e. PPP vis-à-vis traditional contracts/solutions), as explained in Chap. 8. Last but not the least, capital budgeting analyses are applied to calculate the shadow bid, which represents the level of fees/availability charge to be used in tender procedures or in the negotiation with economic operators (EOs).

From a private sector perspective, capital budgeting allows for preparing an offer that, on one hand, best responds to the requirements of the contracting authority (CA) and, on the other hand, adequately remunerates both financial and industrial investors. In other words, it allows for the appraisal of the general viability of a project (the capacity of a project

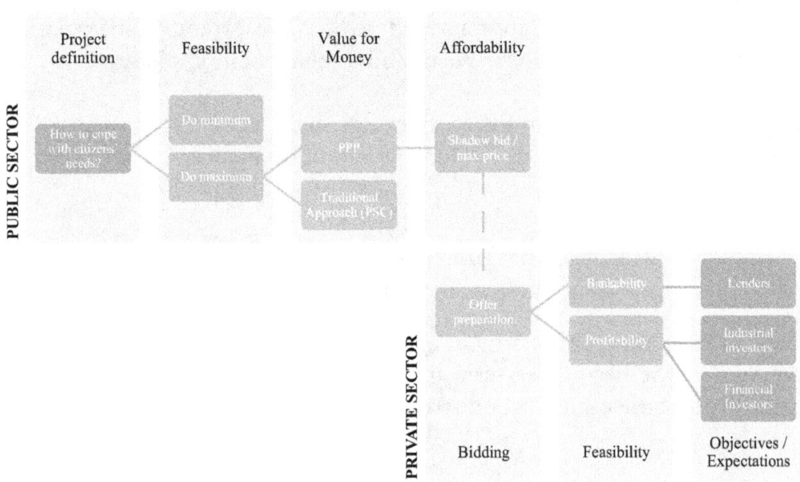

Fig. 7.1 The application of capital budgeting analysis, public and private perspective. Source: Authors

to remunerate production factors employed in the project); the bankability (the capacity of the project to service the debt); and the profitability (the capacity to remunerate the equity invested).

The financial plan is an essential part of a PPP project; therefore, it is not a self-standing document, but must be crafted according to the business model of the project and, above all, the risk allocation.

When both the public authority and the private counterparts develop sound financial analysis for the project, they are able to better craft the contract and reduce the extent of information asymmetry during the procurement and implementation phases.

Many of the drawbacks of existing PPP projects can indeed be explained by weak financial analyses, which generate financial challenges for the public and private sector and the need to renegotiate the contract ex-post to restore an appropriate level of profitability for the private counterpart.

This chapter provides an overview of the essentials of capital budgeting and how to apply these tools to infrastructure financing, providing guidance principles for public managers, investors, and financial analysts.

7.2 Capital Budgeting Tools for Investment Appraisal

When appraising an investment, there are two relevant dimensions to be considered: an economic one and a financial one. The economic dimension provides information about the ability of the project to create or destroy value; its aim is to appraise the balance between the resources drawn and the resources generated by the project. The financial dimension looks at the financial sustainability of the project and examines whether the resources generated are sufficient to pay back the money—both debt and equity—that is used to fund it.

These two dimensions are assessed on the basis of a standard appraising methodology, which consists of the following interlinked types of calculation:

- pro-forma financial plan calculation, which includes a projected profit and loss account, a balance sheet, and a cash flow statement;
- profitability metrics calculation, mainly consisting in net present value (NPV) and internal rate of return (IRR) estimates; and
- cover ratios calculation, which are critical indicators of bankability, that is, the ability of the project to meet lenders' requirements for the term and payment profile of the debt.

In this section we present the main capital budgeting tools, then in Sects. 7.3 and 7.4 we discuss implications for infrastructure financing.

7.2.1 Pro-forma Financial Plan

As shown in Fig. 7.2, the pro-forma financial plan of a project consists of a profit and loss account, a balance sheet, a cash flow statement, and an explanatory note.

Briefly, the profit and loss account provides an overview of project revenues and expenses and shows the net income incurred over a specific accounting period; the balance sheet illustrates a company's financial position at a specific point in time (i.e. the assets owned, shareholders' funds, and liabilities owed); and the cash flow allows the difference between money inflows and outflows of the project to be determined. The explanatory note clarifies the assumptions underlying the calculation of the other financial statements and explains under which conditions the project is economically and financially sustainable, therefore it is not merely an annex, but a fundamental document for understanding the project's dynamics and specifications.

Among the different financial statements, the cash flow statement is the most critical tool when assessing an investment project. In fact, the profit and loss account and balance sheet are calculated on the basis of the accrual method of accounting, under which revenues and expenses are recorded when they are earned, regardless of when the money is actually received or paid. But even profitable projects, as measured by their net incomes, can

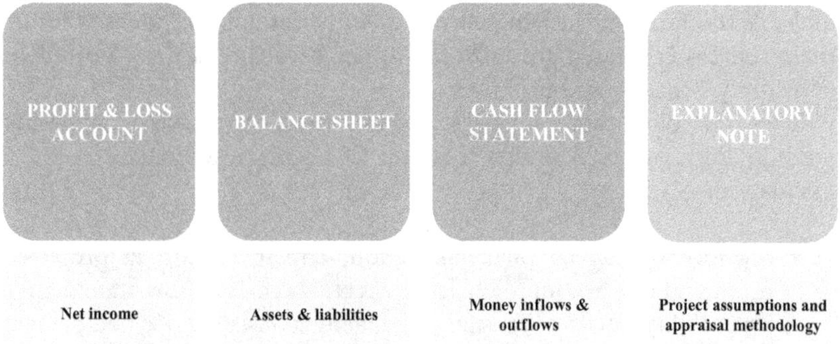

Fig. 7.2 Key documents part of the pro-forma financial plan. Source: Authors

become insolvent if they do not have the cash to settle short-term liabilities. On the contrary, the cash method recognizes inflows when money is received, and outflows when money is paid.

Put simply, a project can be considered economically and financially sound only if the sum of cash outflows is lower than the sum of cash inflows. For this reason, only cash flows are relevant in the assessment of investment projects, such as a PPP contract. This is generally characterized by an investment phase, of one or multiple years, followed by a management phase, where net cash flows should be able to cover and remunerate the upfront investments. The following paragraphs explain the concept of cash flow and how it is determined.

7.2.1.1 Cash Flow Calculation

Any investment project is characterized by a sequence of cash inflows and outflows. Figure 7.3 shows the distribution of cash flows for a typical infrastructure project. In general, cash outflows happen during the construction phase and cash inflows during the management/operation phase. Usually, long-term assets such as new infrastructure facilities generate further value beyond the time horizon used in the assessment, therefore a terminal value can also be considered.

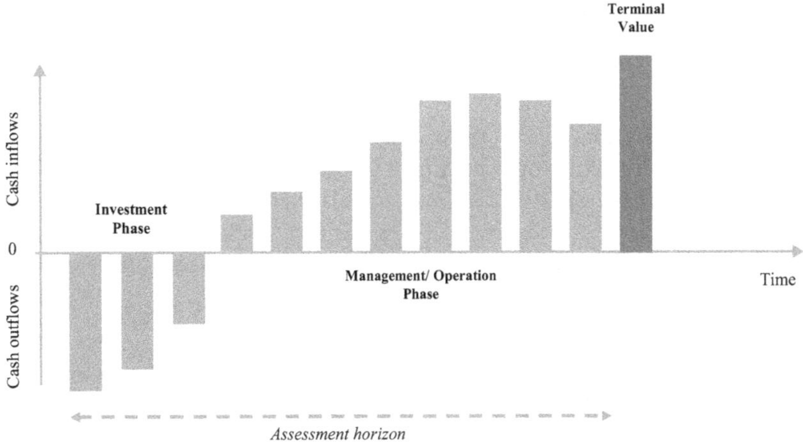

Fig. 7.3 Typical distribution of cash flows of infrastructure projects. Source: Authors

Cash flows in a given period can be calculated following two methods—a direct or indirect method. The main difference between the direct method and the indirect method involves the cash flows from operating activities, which is the first section of cash flow statement. When using the direct method, cash receipts and cash payments from operating activities are listed in the operations section of the cash flow statement. In contrast, in the indirect method, the operating income is derived from the income statement and is adjusted to convert it from an accrual to a cash basis.

Another difference lies in tax calculation. When using the indirect method, taxes derived from the income statement include a tax shield, that is, a reduction that results from taking the interest on debt from taxable income. In contrast, in the direct method, taxes are calculated without deducting the interest on debt, therefore a tax shield is to be included and calculated based on the applicable tax rules (in PPP transactions, the full deductibility of debt interest is usually allowed, therefore the value of a tax shield is calculated as the amount of debt interest, multiplied by the tax rate).

The calculation of cash flows takes on the configuration shown in Fig. 7.4 in every year or every period of the project's life, according to the timing of the cash flows. Generally, the timing of the cash flow statement can be year-based, or six-month based. By determining the difference between money inflows and outflows, the projected cash flow calculation values the ability of the project to create or destroy value (economic dimension) and pay back the money that is used to finance it (financial dimension). These dimensions are assessed, respectively, by two levels of cash flows, that is, the free cash flows to operations (FCFO) and the free cash flows to equity (FCFE). In other words, the FCFO measures the amount of cash generated by the project that can be used to remunerate all the production factors employed in the project, including the financial sources invested (debt and equity); while the FCFE measures the amount of cash that is left to pay equity investors' dividends.

Box 7.1 examines why the FCFE is a more reliable calculation in the context of infrastructure financing compared to other measures, such as the dividend discount model (DDM).

7.2.2 Profitability Metrics: NPV, IRR, and the Appropriate Discount Rates

The main metrics applied to cash flows to assess a project's profitability are the NPV and IRR. Both are measures of profitability; the former expresses it in monetary terms; the latter in percentage (i.e. in relative terms vis-à-vis the cost of the capital invested).

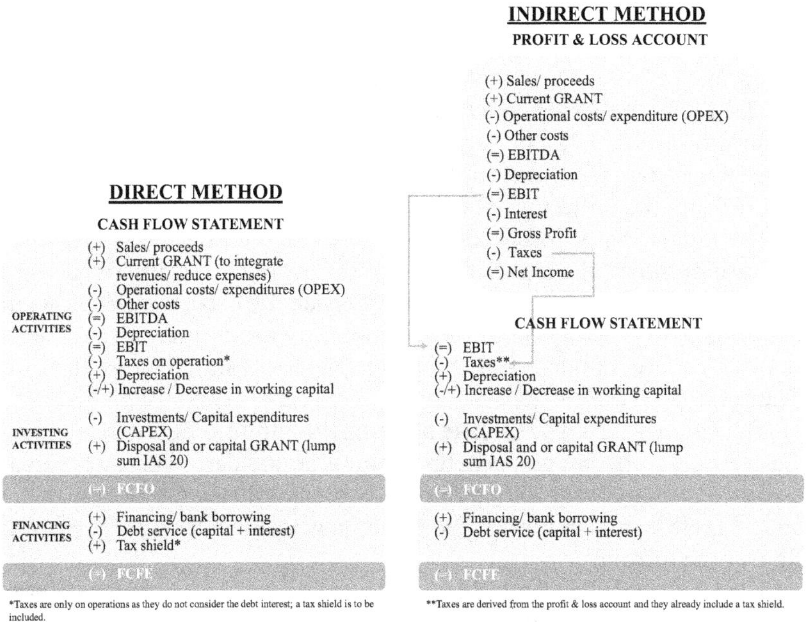

Fig. 7.4 Cash flow calculation using a direct and indirect method. Source: Authors

Box 7.1 FCFE and DDM

Two popular models for valuing equity are the free cash flows to equity (FCFE) and the dividend discount model (DDM). The FCFE values the amount of cash that is left after the debt has been repaid, and it is a measure of what a project can afford to pay out as dividends. The DDM appraises the cash that is actually paid out to sponsors as dividends. Dividends paid can be significantly different from the FCFE for a number of reasons, for example, creation of a debt service reserve amount, future investment needs, tax factors, and so on. The DDM can even be manipulated when dividends are distributed only at the end of the project time horizon with the purpose to reduce the projected return to equity. For its stability, the FCFE offers a more neutral measure of the return to equity compared to the DDM.

A conservative approach can be based on the calculation of the return for equity investors on the basis of FCFE and DDM; however, in the latter, the distribution of dividends shall be forecasted consistently with the most likely disbursements.

These two metrics take into account the time distribution of cash flows, by discounting them at the appropriate cost of capital.

7.2.2.1 The Time Distribution and Value of Cash Flows

As shown in Fig. 7.3, a project's cash flows occur at different times; the time dimension of money outflows and inflows is an essential factor in determining the project profitability.

The longer the period necessary to generate the cash inflows to repay the cash outflows, the higher the risk of the project. The risk is related to the likelihood of the project failing to generate the expected cash flows in the long term. Such risk arises from uncertainty in future cash flow estimates. The level of uncertainty is higher the further in the future the cash flows are.

The risk associated with cash flows in the future reduces their value. Cash flows at different points in time cannot be compared and aggregated, as the immediate availability of money is preferred to a future availability and, therefore, a cash flow in the future is worth less than a similar cash flow in the present.

The principle of present value (PV) enables us to calculate exactly how much a cash flow sometime in the future is worth in today's money and to move cash flows across time. The process of converting future cash flows into cash flows in present value terms is called discounting. This process allows for bringing all cash flows to "period 0," as if they were at the same point in time, before comparing and aggregating them.

As we discuss below, both the NPV and IRR apply the discounting process to evaluate project profitability.

7.2.2.2 NPV

The NPV expresses the net value generated by a project and it is based on the discounted cash flow calculation.

The NPV is the sum of the present values of all the future cash flows generated by the project. As it considers not only the positive cash flows (usually generated during the management/operation phase), but also the outflows (generated during the construction phase), the NPV shows the difference between the project's financial benefits and costs, expressed in current money terms.

A positive NPV means that the project is able to generate enough resources to pay for the investment carried out and the cost of financial resources, while leaving free cash flow for further investments or the remuneration of shareholders. Therefore, the NPV rule implies that a project with an NPV ≥ 0 is worth undertaking—for example is accretive to the value of the business—while one with an NPV < 0 is not.

The NPV can be computed by making use of MS Excel, as shown in Fig. 7.5.

The choice of discount rate is crucial in determining the value of the project as an investment; the higher the rate, the lower the NPV, and *vice versa*. Figure 7.6 shows the NPV function, where K* is the discount rate that makes the NPV equal to zero. K* is the maximum cost of financial resources that the project, with a certain distribution of cash flows, can afford.

7.2.2.3 IRR

The IRR measures the return, expressed as a percentage, on the investment over its life. The NPV and the IRR are related to each other, as the IRR is the discount rate at which the NPV of the cash flow is zero. The

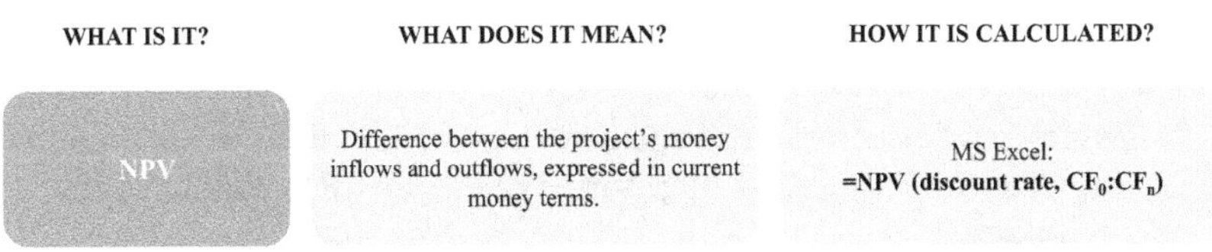

Fig. 7.5 NPV calculation. Source: Authors

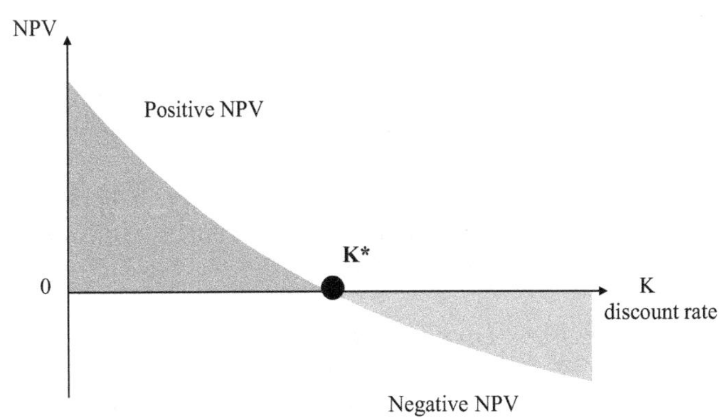

Fig. 7.6 The NPV and discount rate function. Source: Authors

WHAT IS IT?	WHAT DOES IT MEAN?	HOW IT IS CALCULATED?
IRR	Return, expressed as a percentage, generated by the project's money inflows and outflows.	MS Excel: **=IRR (CF_0:CF_n)**

Fig. 7.7 IRR calculation. Source: Authors

IRR is, then, equal to the discount rate K* (as shown in Fig. 7.6) and it expresses the maximum cost of the financial resources that the project, with a certain distribution of cash flows, can afford.

The IRR can be computed by making use of MS Excel, as shown in Fig. 7.7.

If the IRR generated by the project is higher than the discount rate, the project generates incremental value. In contrast, if the IRR is lower than the discount rate, the development of the project faces financial costs that are higher than those it can afford.

It must be noted that the use of IRR for investment appraisal has three main pitfalls, namely:

- Multiple rates of return: in the case of positive cash flows followed by negative ones and then by positive ones, the IRR may have multiple values.
- Mutually exclusive projects: IRR should not be used to rate mutually exclusive projects, as it ignores the magnitude of the project and for certain cash flows, in a comparison of investments, the higher IRR does not represent a higher NPV.
- Term structure assumption: the use of IRR falsely assumes that discount rates are stable during the term of the project; this assumption implies that all interim cash flows are reinvested at the same IRR.

In general, NPV and IRR produce the same investment decision, but this is not always the case, and NPV is generally regarded as more robust, as a consequence of the IRR's weaknesses.

7.2.2.4 The Appropriate Discount Rates

The choice of "most appropriate discount" rate is key to determining the profitability of a project, and this rate corresponds to the opportunity cost of capital.

As we discuss in Sect. 7.4, the NPV and IRR can be calculated both at project level and for equity investors. At project level, NPV and IRR are calculated on the FCFO; the discount rate to be used is the *weighted average cost of capital* (hereafter, WACC). For equity investors, NPV and IRR are calculated on the FCFE; the discount rate to be used is the *cost of equity* (Ke).

Section 7.3.2 presents the methodology to calculate the cost of capital for infrastructure projects.

7.2.3 Cover Ratios: DSCR

Along with profitability, any project should also be valued in terms of bankability. In other words, a project can be profitable but might not be bankable if the timing of the operating cash flows does not match the needs of lenders for debt service payment. Moreover, a project can generate a given NPV and IRR with various cash flow combinations, but these mixes are not always acceptable to lenders.

Cover ratios are indicators of bankability and are the most important examples of financial covenants included in the credit agreement. Cover ratios are indices that can show the extent to which a project's operating cash flows match those linked to the dynamic of financial liabilities.

A number of cover ratios are currently in use; among them, the *debt service cover ratio* (DSCR) is commonly applied. The DSCR is calculated annually and expresses the relation between the FCFO and the debt service on the principal and interest, as shown in Fig. 7.8. In other words, the ratio expresses whether, in any given year of operations, the financial resources generated by the project are able to cover the debt service to lenders.

If the DSCR is higher than 1 it means that the cash flows of the project are sufficient to pay back the debt service; if it is lower than 1 it means that the resources generated by the project are not able to repay the debt.

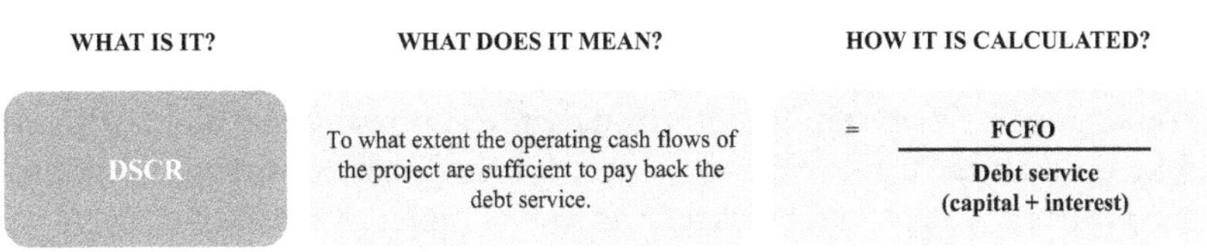

Fig. 7.8 DCSR calculation. Source: Authors

Observed levels of DSCR depend on the deal—that is, the risk inherent to the project as perceived by lenders. However, in general, the material breach of covenants is frequently associated with DSCR close to 1.03x–1.05x.

It must be noted that, in the case of project financing, the debt repayment obligations are typically calculated to ensure that the principal and interests are appropriately matched to achieve a desired target DSCR—which is usually referred to as debt sculpting.

7.3 Applying Capital Budgeting Tools to Infrastructure Financing

The application of capital budgeting principles to infrastructure investing and particularly to PPP requires some specific considerations, which are the focus of this section.

Compared to other investment projects, the planning of infrastructure represents a complex and interdisciplinary process for a number of reasons. First, it is characterized by high information uncertainty. During early planning stages, the majority of technical as well as economic parameters, which are of crucial importance for the detailed design and project implementation, cannot be determined with precision. In addition, PPP infrastructure projects are based on agreements signed with a public authority according to which the risk is limited vis-à-vis a pure private investment, as some risks are retained by the CA (as discussed in Chap. 5).

Therefore, it is fundamental to accurately calculate the pro-forma financial plan by making credible and realistic assumptions about key input parameters. Relying on historical data (if available) and market data, as well as performing sensitivities, reduces the range of uncertainties resulting from an information deficit. In addition, *the assessment of the cost of capital is essential to set the appropriate level of profitability for the level of risk embedded in the project.*

7.3.1 Modelling of Key Input Data

From an operational standpoint, to apply the appraising methodology and come up with the estimation of expected future cash flow of an infrastructure project, a set of input variables is to be defined, such as:

- the timing of the investment and the appraisal horizon;
- investment costs (capex);
- changes in working capital;
- public grants (when available);
- the financial structure and the mix of funding sources;
- analysis of operating costs (opex) and revenues during the operating life of the project;
- macroeconomic variables, including inflation, taxes, and the value-added tax (VAT) dynamic (if VAT is imposed in a given country).

7.3.1.1 The Timing of the Investment and the Appraisal Horizon

The choice of the time horizon for which forecasts are provided depends on two elements: the economic lifetime of the asset and the duration (maturity) of the underlying sources of financing (with particular reference to senior debt). This choice is key as it affects the appraisal results.

The lifetime of a project is generally shorter when it requires investments in assets that are technology intensive, therefore subject to a rapid obsolescence; as noted in Chap. 4, the inclusion of technology refresh should be carefully considered. For projects with large investments in hard infrastructure, the economic lifetime of the asset can be very long, and it is generally not possible to match this timeframe with a reasonable appraisal horizon (see Box 7.2). This is also due to the maximum duration of the sources of financing available on the market (the senior debt provided by banks is usually to be repaid in a maximum of 20 years, which can be extended up to 30 years when long-term investors such as development banks are involved).

Box 7.2 Longer time horizons do not increase the financial sustainability and bankability of a project

If a project does not reach the financial sustainability and bankability within the selected horizon, it is not worth extending the appraisal timeframe and the concession contract length (also discussed in Sect. 7.3.1.1). This is due to the process of discounting (see Sect. 7.2.2.1), for which, beyond a certain time horizon, future cash inflows have a limited impact on the profitability metrics of the project. In this case, it is rather recommendable to adjust other project input variables, such as revenues and operating costs, or the amount of public grants.

Table 7.1 European Commission's reference periods by sector

Sector	*Reference period (years)*
Railways	30
Roads	25–30
Ports and airports	25
Urban transport	25–30
Water supply/sanitation	30
Waste management	25–30
Energy	15–25
Broadband	15–20
Healthcare and other social infrastructure	20–25
Research and innovation	15–25
Business infrastructure	10–15
Other sectors	10–15

Source: ANNEX I to Commission Delegated Regulation (EU) No 480/2014

In practice, it is therefore helpful to refer to standard benchmarks, differentiated by sector and based on internationally accepted practice. In the European Union, the Commission-proposed reference periods are shown in Table 7.1. These values should be considered as including the construction/implementation period. In the case of unusually long construction periods, longer values can be adopted. However, the choice of the length of a contract and therefore the appraisal horizon should be crafted according to the specific features of the project and its context.

When the appraisal horizon is shorter than the economic lifetime of the asset, a terminal value of the fixed investments must be included within the investment costs account for the year-end. The terminal value reflects the capacity of the remaining service potential of fixed assets whose economic life is not yet completely exhausted. The latter will be zero or negligible if a time horizon equal to the economic lifetime of the asset has been selected. The terminal value must be carefully considered. As a matter of fact, in a PPP contract the investment is, generally, entirely depreciated within the life of the contract (by using a straight-line depreciation, as discussed in Sect. 7.3.1.2). If there is a terminal value, the CA has to pay the terminal value to the EO when the contract expires. Terminal value can be applied in feasibility analysis, in the comparison between alternative scenarios, such as the do-minimum and the do-maximum. In these circumstances, when the same time horizon is adopted for the two options to be compared, a terminal value can be considered in the do-maximum scenario, since the do-maximum investment is able to generate a value for the CA (and for society also) beyond the appraisal period.

The terminal value can be determined in multiple ways: (i) by computing the net present value of future cash flows in the remaining life years of the assets; (ii) by computing the residual value of the asset based on a standard accounting depreciation formula; or (iii) by considering the residual market value of the fixed asset as if it were to be sold at the end of the time horizon.

7.3.1.2 Investment Costs (capex)

Investment costs include initial investments and replacement costs.

Initial investments include the capital costs of all the fixed assets (e.g. land, constructions buildings, plant and machinery, equipment, etc.) and non-fixed assets (e.g. start-up and technical costs such as design/planning, project management and technical assistance, construction supervision, publicity, etc.). Where appropriate, rolled-up interest and senior debt fees (e.g. the agency fee and the commitment fee) should also be included. Information must be taken from the technical feasibility study. Cost breakdown over the years should be consistent with the physical realizations envisaged and the time-plan for implementation.

Replacement costs include costs occurring during the reference time horizon to replace short-life technologies and/or equipment. It is preferable not to compute cash flows for large replacements close to the end of the appraisal horizon. When a specific project asset needs to be replaced shortly before the end of the reference time horizon, the timeframe can be shortened to match the end of the lifetime of the asset that needs replacing. As an alternative, if appropriate, the replacement can be postponed until after the end of the reference time horizon and assume an increase of the annual maintenance and repair cost for the specific asset until the end of the project.

Usually, depreciation of initial investments and replacement costs are calculated by adopting a straight-line approach, by depreciating the entire amount across the reference time horizon.

7.3.1.3 Changes in Working Capital

Changes in net working capital should also be included in the analysis, where appropriate. Increase in working capital from one period to another reduces the project's cash flows, and *vice versa*. For example, if the project's accounts receivable increase at the end of the year, this means that less money is collected compared to what is recorded in sales during the same year. On the flip side, if accounts payable are also to increase, it means a project is able to pay its suppliers more slowly, which is positive for cash flow.

It must be noted that, due to the long-term horizon of infrastructure projects, changes in working capital can be negligible, as periodical increases compensate for periodical decreases in working capital in the long run.

7.3.1.4 Public Grants

The availability of public grants is quite common in the context of infrastructure financing, especially for those projects that are particularly capital intensive.

Public grants, when available, optimize the financial sustainability and bankability of a project because they reduce the need of private capitals. The period in which the grant is paid is also relevant. If it is paid during the investment phase, the costs associated with rolled up interest are lower; if it is paid at the delivery of the infrastructure, there is the need to finance the total capital costs with private capitals (equity and debt), with any consequent increase in rolled-up interests.

The money to be injected in the form of grant could become available as a consequence of the sale of public assets, that is, facilities replaced by the new infrastructure built. In this case, the grant is paid by the CA during the management phase and, in general, the money received by the SPV/EO is used to reimburse part of the debt (preferably the shareholder loan or also the senior debt).

7.3.1.5 The Financial Structure and the Mix of Funding Sources

Infrastructure projects are financed through a mix of debt and equity (see Chap. 2). On the debt side, besides senior debt, other forms of junior debt (such as "mezzanine" debt) or a shareholder loan can be used. In general, the financial structure shall be designed to optimize the cost of finance for the project and is usually highly leveraged.

The debt repayment profile can be flat (i.e. following a regular amortization approach, such as the French or the Italian one; this is usually applied in the case of corporate financing) or designed to meet the lender's covenants (i.e. applying the so-called debt sculpting; this also is usually applied in the case of project financing).

The choices regarding the mix of funding sources affect the cost of capital (see Sect. 7.3.2 below) and the appraisal results.

7.3.1.6 *Analysis of Operating Costs and Revenues During the Operating Life of the Project*

Operating costs include all the costs for operating the service and maintaining the infrastructure. They are often referred to with the term Operation & Maintenance (O&M). Cost forecasts can be based on historic unit costs, when patterns of operations and maintenance expenditure ensured adequate quality standards. Although the actual composition is project-specific, typical O&M costs include: labor costs for the employer; materials needed for maintenance and repair of assets; consumption of raw materials, fuel, energy, and other process consumables; services purchased from third parties, rent of buildings or sheds, rental of machinery; general management and administration; insurance costs; quality control; and waste disposal costs.

O&M costs correspond to the price of services sold by the subcontractors to the SPV, therefore O&M costs shall include an industrial mark-up (even when subcontractors are the same industrial sponsors of the SPV). However, while including the appropriate mark-up, these costs shall not be fully adjusted for the risks that may accrue to the project, otherwise incentives for efficient and effective management are reduced (as discussed in Sect. 7.4).

Operating revenues are represented by tariffs, shadow tolls, and/or availability payments, and correspond to the amount of revenue that is needed to reach the economic and financial equilibrium. From an operational point of view, they shall be computed by making use of the "goal seek function" of MS Excel.

Forecasted revenues, while sustaining the feasibility, bankability, and profitability of the project, shall leave the appropriate incentive to the investors to monitor and manage risks.

7.3.1.7 *Macroeconomic Variables*

Among macroeconomic variables, the choice of inflation has a key impact on cash flows that are dynamic in the medium to long term.

The pro-forma financial plan should usually be carried out in constant (real) prices, that is, with prices fixed at a base-year, for those items that are not subject to inflation. This is particularly true for investment costs in mature economies, given the relatively short time requested for implementation. The use of current (nominal) prices, that is, prices adjusted by the Consumer Price Index (CPI), is usually applied to O&M costs. Operating revenues shall be partially adjusted by inflation, considering only the portion of revenues that is needed to cover O&M expenses (thus excluding the portion that covers investment costs).

The application of inflation involves an estimation of future CPI. Long-term inflation forecasts provided by central banks and international financial institutions can be considered a reliable source to estimate such a value.

7.3.2 Cost of Capital

The calculation of the opportunity cost of capital is essential in order to set the appropriate level of profitability and safeguard the affordability of an infrastructure project.

The funds used to invest in infrastructure projects have other potential uses in the economy. Therefore, in theory, holders of such funds will invest in a given project only if the return they expect to earn from doing so exceeds the market price of the risk involved. The cost of capital is determined by the amount of risk it is perceived to involve and the market price of that risk. Therefore, how the market perceives risk and how it prices that risk are fundamental issues that we must address in generating an estimate of the cost of capital.

From an operational point of view, the calculation of the cost of capital requires the calculation of the WACC, which takes into consideration both the cost of equity (Ke) and the cost of debt (Kd), with weights represented by the optimal debt-to-equity (or gearing) ratio, as shown in Fig. 7.9.

It must be noted that, in the context of infrastructure project appraisal, the debt-to-equity ratio is not stable over the entire life of the project but rapidly decreases as the debt is reimbursed. Therefore, the WACC changes and should be calculated in every period. However, conventionally, the project WACC can be calculated using the project average debt-to-equity ratio.

If the financial structure also includes a mezzanine debt/shareholder loan, the WACC formula should be amended accordingly, thus including the share of such further financial source and its cost.

The Kd is typically the sum of a reference rate (e.g. federal funds rate in the US, Euribor, and Eurirs in the European Union) plus a floating spread,

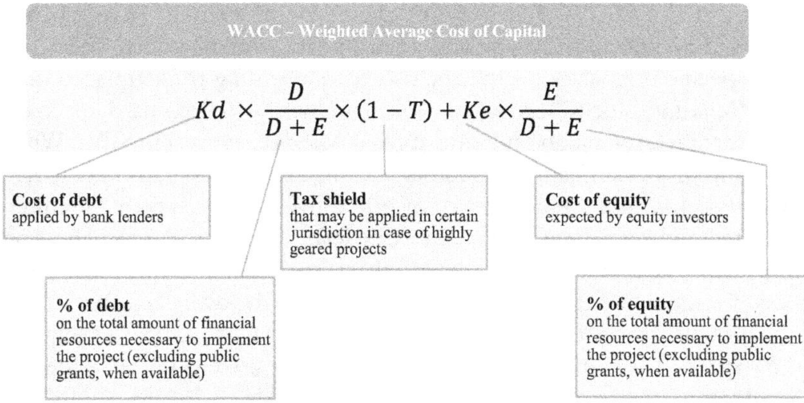

Fig. 7.9 WACC calculation. Source: Authors

which reflects the financial market's perception of the project's inherent risk as well as the intensity of competition in the financial markets. Therefore, this cost depends on project features (especially in cases of project financing), such as the economic/financial soundness of the initiative and the level of risk coverage provided by the contractual network surrounding the deal.

The Ke is the expected return by equity providers. While Kd is a market value and therefore easily known, Ke is more difficult to calculate. It expresses, in theory, the average return that could have been earned by putting the same amount of money into a different investment with equal risk.

For listed companies, Ke is defined (according to the Capital Asset Pricing Model theory [CAPM]—a method commonly used by firms to determine the minimum acceptable return on investment) as the sum of (i) the rate of return available on risk-free investments (the risk-free rate) and (ii) a premium for the amount of systematic risk that is involved in the equity investment (the Equity Risk Premium) (Graham and Harvey 2002).

For infrastructure transactions, the cost of the equity invested is calculated by using different methodologies, depending on the nature of the investor (industrial or financial) and type of investment (direct or indirect, in the latter case the investment is intermediated by setting up the SPV).

Industrial investors tend to quote the cost of the equity by using their weighted average cost of capital as a hurdle rate, and, if needed, they consider specific premiums for specific risk factors, adding these up according to a "building blocks" approach. This approach is the standard approach for direct investment, and it is also applied when they invest in SPVs. When investing in SPVs, financial investors tend to use a comparative approach, by considering the average return of other investments as their minimum expected return. These approaches can lead to incorrect estimates and sometimes to overpricing the expected return, thus affecting the general value for money of the transaction for the CA or the overall society.

The CAPM can be considered the orthodox approach for estimating the cost of the equity of PPP when an SPV is set up, even if SPVs are not listed (Box 7.3 illustrates how to apply the CAPM).

Box 7.3 The cost of equity in PPP infrastructure projects

The degree of risk involved in an investment determines the cost of capital. Finance theory refers to two main categories of risk which require distinct analysis: these are specific (or idiosyncratic) risk; and systematic (or market) risk.

Specific risks are associated with events that affect the cash flows of the individual project under evaluation, but not the cash flows of other assets in an investor's portfolio. This means that the overall portfolio returns for the investor are unaffected, especially if the investor's portfolio is adequately diversified. Therefore, specific risks must be taken into consideration, by adjusting the expected cash flows, not as a premium on the cost of equity. Most of the technical risks associated with PPPs pertain to this latter type of risk. Further, when the SPV is set up, these risks are often transferred to subcontractors and therefore they do not affect the return of the single investment.

In contrast, systematic risks are those that are correlated with the overall performance of the stock market or the general economy, and they affect the majority of assets in an investor's portfolio. For this reason, they have a direct effect on portfolio returns. Risks in this category include: the costs of inputs (especially those commodities sold on international markets), regional or global political instability, demand risk, and various types of financing risk. They can be diversified neither at portfolio level, nor within a single project. Therefore,

(*continued*)

Box 7.3 (continued)

they should be adequately considered in the estimation of the cost of the equity, or in other words in the expected return for investors.

As noted, the CAPM represents the reference framework for estimating the cost of the equity for PPP transactions. Under CAPM the opportunity cost of equity is equal to the return on risk-free securities plus an Equity Risk Premium, which is the product of two variables:

- the Beta of the investment—the weighted covariance of the forecast excess return on the project with the average excess return on the whole market (it is the key measure of systematic risk); and
- the Equity Market Risk Premium (EMRP)—the average premium above the risk-free rate on equities, reflecting the amount of risk in the equity market portfolio.

The risk-free rate is the return on an investment with no variance around the expected return. It is standard practice to use government security rates to estimate risk-free rates, and the selection of the appropriate security rate is a function of the expected holding period for the investment to which the discount rate is to apply. In PPP contracts, by their long-run horizon, the yield on long-term government bond—that is, 10-year, 20-year, or 30-year—is commonly used. The geographical location of the project does not determine the choice of the risk-free interest rate. Rather, this is determined by the currency in which the cash flows are to be estimated

Estimates of the ERPM are not uniform across global equity markets, as they depend on:

- the period over which returns are calculated;
- the method chosen for computing the average rates of return; and
- whether they are set to reflect current or expected market conditions.

Nevertheless, the most widely used methodology to estimate ERPM is the so-called historical risk premium approach, where the average return earned on equities over a long time period is estimated and compared to the average return on a risk-free security. The difference, on an annual basis, between the two returns is com-

(continued)

Box 7.3 (continued)

puted using the arithmetic or geometric average. This difference represents the historical risk premium.

This is a relatively straightforward process for mature markets but presents a number of challenges when the analysis is focused on markets with short and/or volatile histories. This is clearly true for emerging markets, in which historical data are either non-existent or unreliable and where a few large companies (many of them unlisted) may be dominant.

Once the ERPM is obtained, more difficult challenges are presented when deriving the appropriate Beta for a PPP investment.

Beta can be easily estimated for those projects that are developed by listed EOs; this is the case of network infrastructures (road, oil and gas, energy), since the EOs' core business is actually infrastructure building and operation. In such circumstances, the sector average Beta is used, calculated at national or supranational level. An average supranational Beta can be considered only if economic and political geographies are consistent with the project's context.

For sectors in which financing with private capitals is a novelty, such as healthcare, or when the project perimeter encompasses several businesses, estimating the Beta can be more difficult. In such cases, two approaches can be used:

- Beta can be estimated by using the Beta(s) of businesses exposed to similar systematic risks; for example, the Beta of utilities can be applied to healthcare investments because they both face a rigid demand, which is the main determinant of systematic risk.
- Beta can be estimated by using the Beta(s) from industries or firms with similar activities to those undertaken in the PPP project and are thus exposed to the similar risks (weighting these Betas for the specific weight of correspondent activities in the project). In such cases, some adjustments (by adding or subtracting risk factors) are needed because the risks retained by investors in traditional business may be higher than those retained in a PPP contract; adjustments are also needed for emerging markets, where PPP contracts may be particularly risky.

A set of relevant sectors is provided in Table 7.2. This shows average asset Betas for four industries in Europe, where regulatory and economic features are fairly standard across Western European countries. To provide an example, we use the average Beta of four such sectors, but different approaches can be considered, as explained above.

(*continued*)

Box 7.3 (continued)

Table 7.2 Average asset Betas for selected industries in Europe, adjusted by Blume

Sector	*Beta sector*
Infrastructure construction	0.790
Railroad	0.601
Real estate owners and developers	0.650
Utilities (average)	0.630
Utilities (power generation)	0.678
Utilities (networks)	0.496
Utilities (water)	0.566

Source: Damodaran online http://pages.stern.nyu.edu/~adamodar/

We have included the regulated utilities sector as well as the (more intuitive) construction, railroad, and real estate sectors, because PPPs can expect to:

- incur high capital investments;
- experience low volatility in demand (esp. if payments are availability based);
- have relatively predictable costs; and
- have long time horizons.

If sector Beta is not available, it is possible to create a basket of comparable companies and derive the Beta from them. The risk in such cases is to have limited baskets of comparable companies and therefore adjustments must be applied.

Our source for data is Damodaran online but other sources include the Bloomberg, Thomson Datastream, and OneBanker databases.

It should be noted that the form of a company's Beta that is available in these databases is the Equity Beta. This form of Beta reflects the level of systematic risk that a company's shareholders face in addition to risks relating to the firm's financial leverage (which will be different to the leverage of the specific project under consideration). Therefore, in this table, the Equity Betas of the companies from which the raw data have been extracted are turned into "unleveraged" or Asset Betas through the use of the standard formula:

Asset Beta = Equity Beta ÷ [1 + (1 - tax rate) × (amount of debt ÷ amount of equity)].

(*continued*)

Box 7.3 (continued)

Table 7.3 Cost of equity calculation for a PPP project in Germany

	Value
Risk-free rate (government 10YR bond yield)	0.054%
Equity Risk Premium	5.395%
ERPM	5.230%
Asset Beta (as calculated in Table 7.2)	0.630
Re-levered Beta	1.032
Tax rate	15.00%
Leverage D/E	75.00%
Total benchmark cost of equity	5.449%

Betas are adjusted according to Blume theory (Blume 1971) to reflect the fact that estimated Betas have a tendency to revert to the market mean (i.e. 1) over time.[1]

This Beta provides no more than a starting point for estimating the Beta for PPP investors. To turn this into an appropriate Beta for the derivation of the Equity Risk Premium, the asset Beta is re-leveraged according to the leverage of the specific project.[2]

Table 7.3 shows the calculation of the cost of the equity by applying the CAPM methodology to a PPP project in Germany (considering an average leverage for the PPP project of 75%).

For more details on the cost of the equity calculation with specific reference to emerging countries, a synthesis is included in Hellowell and Vecchi (2018).

[1] The effect of the Blume adjustment is to reduce the difference between the Beta and the market average (i.e. 1). Blume (1971) found that adjusting estimated Equity Betas toward unity improved their ability to forecast subsequent period stock returns. The most widely held explanation for this is that unusually low or high Betas are subject to measurement error. Blume adjustment is standard in the calculation of Equity Betas by regulators in respect of UK, US, and Australian utilities in determining the appropriate rate of return to investors, and is recommended in the most prominent corporate finance textbooks (e.g. Brealey et al. 2019). Blume-adjusted Betas are available from most commercial databases, such as Bloomberg and the London Business School Risk Management Service. The formula is: Blume-adjusted Equity Beta = (0.67)* βOLS + (0.33)*1.

[2] In effect, reversing the process in which the sectoral Asset Betas were derived from the observable *Equity Betas*, thus: *Equity Beta* = *Asset Beta* × 1 + (1 - tax rate) × the amount of debt ÷ the amount of equity.

If the project is also financed with mezzanine debt and/or a shareholder loan, it is fundamental to price correctly this further financial source. In general, the risk attached to such an "intermediate" layer is higher than that associated with debt and lower compared to equity. One of the most common mistakes is to use the same cost of the capital for the pure equity and the shareholder loan. Actually, this is wrong because a shareholder loan has a lower risk profile, that is, it is more flexible and can be prioritized in the reimbursement, while the equity shall remain invested in the SPV till the contract expires.

7.3.3 Sensitivities

The pro-forma financial plan also needs to be sufficiently flexible to allow both the CA and private investors to calculate a series of sensitivities showing the effects of variations in the key input assumptions. Such sensitivities may include calculating the effect on profitability metrics and cover ratios of:

- construction-cost overrun;
- delay in completion;
- deductions or penalties for failure to meet availability or service requirements;
- reduced usage of the project (where private investors assume demand risk);
- higher opex and maintenance costs;
- higher cost of the debt (where it is not fixed);
- changes in inflation.

In summary, the sensitivities look at the financial effect of the commercial- and financial- risk aspects of the project not working out as originally expected. This calculation of several different adverse events happening at once is also called scenario analysis.

Sensitivities are very important for understanding the capacity of the project to face risks. Investors should be aware of the impact of risks on the project profitability. At the same time, the public sector should check that the project cash flows are not fully adjusted to the risk, otherwise the private investors have no incentive to manage the project in a way to avoid risk appearance and therefore to successfully execute the PPP contract, in order to generate value per se and for the taxpayers.

In the context of the European Union, these calculations also serve the purpose of demonstrating the transfer to the concessionaire of an operating risk, as discussed in Chap. 5.

7.4 Appraising Infrastructure Investments: The Concept of Economic and Financial Equilibrium

As discussed in Sect. 7.2.2, when considering an investment, private investors generally use NPV and IRR to assess the general financial profitability of a project. Further, they use the opportunity cost of capital as a "hurdle rate," choosing those investments whose IRR is at least equal or above the opportunity cost of capital, in which case the NPV is also positive.

However, PPP projects are based on agreements signed with CAs based on a clear level of risks transfer, which is essential to create incentives on private investors. Therefore, at the time of contract signature, the project must ensure the economic and financial equilibrium, which means that project revenues (tariffs, shadow tolls, or availability charges) shall be enough to cover:

- operating and capital costs, also including the industrial investors' margins;
- interest on debt;
- taxes;
- dividends forecasted on the basis of the expected return for equity investors.

The economic and financial equilibrium is reached if the conditions shown in Fig. 7.10 are met.

If such conditions are not met and when traditional corporate finance investment decisions are applied (based on NPV > 0 and IRR > the cost of the capital), the risk allocation can be compromised. Actually, projected cash flows generate higher return than the fair level, based on the risks borne by investors. Since risks estimates are difficult, both idiosyncratic and systemic, the tendency among investors is to neglect the application of the economic and financial equilibrium rule, which is mandatory for CAs since it ensures effective risks allocation.

Of course, the application of such condition requires a rigorous approach, both in the estimates of the cash flows components and in the cost of the equity.

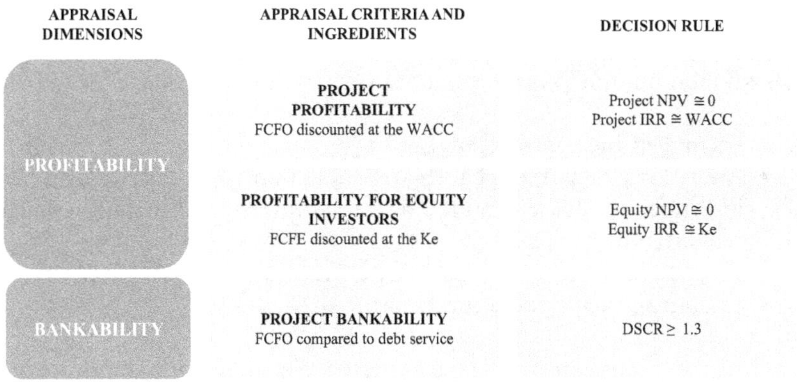

Fig. 7.10 The conditions of economic and financial equilibrium. Source: Authors

7.5 Contract Renegotiation Using Capital Budgeting Tools

Many PPP contracts are renegotiated during the operational phase. This is more likely than in other contract types because of the length and complexity of such deals. In general, renegotiations threaten the public sector's financial position. Yet a renegotiation may be necessary when factors outside the responsibility of the SPV occur that generate losses. In this case the renegotiation is called by the SPV itself. It is also possible that the authority calls for a renegotiation if these facts generate extra revenues for the SPV, that is, in case of more favorable taxation or changes in the law.

The most frequent renegotiations happen as a consequence of the need for different investments than those planned during the construction phase. Renegotiations may be dictated also when the financial conditions of the SPV are deteriorated as a consequence of wrong projections, for example if the demand has been overestimated. This is an extraordinary case and the CA may decide to enter into renegotiation to preserve the project which is generally associated with the achievement of public interest. If the SPV should go bankrupt, losses are not only faced by investors but also by the community.

Renegotiation implies the preparation of a new financial plan, changing only the input data that dictate the renegotiation itself, while leaving all the other values unaltered. The amended financial plan will show a different NPV and IRR compared to those agreed upon at the time of contract signature. Therefore, in order to restore the economic and financial equilibrium, the following solutions could be considered:

- Change in the contract length
- Award of a capital grant if the renegotiation takes place during the investment phase and further investments have been requested by the CA
- Increase in the level of availability charge
- Change in the payment mechanism.

Other solutions could also be considered, depending on the features of the project.

The contract renegotiation process becomes challenging when the original pro-forma financial statements lack transparency or are not clearly developed, or when the circumstances that have led to the renegotiation are multiple and accumulated over time.

References

Blume, M. E. (1971). On the Assessment of Risk, The Journal of Finance, March, pp. 1-10.

Brealey, R., Myers, S., & Allen, F. (2019). *Principles of Corporate Finance*. 13th Edition, McGraw Hill.

Graham, J., & Harvey, C. (2002). The Theory and Practice of Corporate Finance: Evidence from the Field. *Journal of Financial Economics, 60*, 60–78.

Hellowell, M., & Vecchi, V. (2018). *Assessing the Cost of Capital for PPP Contracts. In Public-Private Partnerships in Health* (pp. 85–109). Cham: Palgrave Macmillan.

CHAPTER 8

Value for Money Analysis: Standard and Value-based Methodologies

Veronica Vecchi and Niccolò Cusumano

Abstract This chapter describes the role of Value for Money Analysis (VfMA), to compare the value generated by PPP contracts vis-à-vis traditional procurement contracts or solutions for contracting authorities. After describing the traditional methodology firstly introduced in Anglo-Saxon countries to assess availability-fee contracts and discusses its limits the chapter introduces a new approach to measure the value generated by PPP contracts, which incorporates the social dimension, that is, the value generated for the society. This approach is also more consistent with the shift toward more environmental and social sustainability undertaken by many private companies and the need for PPP contracts to provide new solutions to societal challenges.

Keywords Value for money • Methodologies • Public sector comparator • Risk quantification • Cost benefit analysis

8.1 Evaluating Public Projects and Programs

Governments and multilateral institutions around the world require programs/projects that apply for funding, especially infrastructure ones, to be economically, environmentally, and socially sustainable in order to ensure

V. Vecchi et al., *Public Private Partnerships*,
https://doi.org/10.1007/978-3-030-65435-1_8

that their operations comply with broad objectives of inclusive economic growth, environmental sustainability, and regional integration.

Financial evaluation is an important part of infrastructure projects' assessment. However, indications of financial sustainability do not necessarily provide reliable estimates of the value of a project from a "social" point of view. Therefore, it is fundamental for public authorities to combine economic and financial assessment.

The purpose of economic evaluation is to assess the value a project generates for society as a whole and consists in conducting a comparative analysis between different alternatives in terms of both costs and consequences of the actions undertaken (Drummond et al. 2015). The word "social" is often used in the literature to denote the idea that in the assessment are included the effects of the project on all the individuals in society, and not just those related to the parties directly involved.

That said, when appraising a project/program, the analyst shall provide the decision-maker with the elements to address two questions:

1. In a context of limited resources, what project alternative can deliver better financial, economic, environmental, and social returns on investment, and therefore is to be preferred?
2. Once a project is selected, which way of delivery offers the best value for money?

In order to answer the first question, we should compare the resources necessary to carry out a project (i.e. costs) and its results measured in terms of impact, outcome, or benefit. Each dimension corresponds to a different evaluation technique.

Cost-effectiveness analysis (CEA) assesses effectiveness by comparing project costs and impact defined as a medium-term change directly related to the tangible results (i.e. the relation between outputs and outcomes) of the intervention. CEA focuses on a single dimension of effectiveness and reports on it in natural units. It aims to select the project that, for a given level of effectiveness, minimizes the net present value of costs or, alternatively, for a given cost, maximizes the effectiveness level.

Cost-utility analysis (CUA) also measures project effectiveness but in terms of preferences expressed by individuals or society regarding the achievement of a certain outcome. Compared to CEA, CUA does not consider outcomes in absolute, but in relative terms since it incorporates individual preferences.

Multi-criteria analysis (MCA) includes multiple criteria, simultaneously considering quantitative and qualitative data, and multiple stakeholders.

In a cost-benefit analysis (CBA) cost and impact of a particular project are estimated and converted into monetary terms. Compared to a CEA and a CUA, CBA allows for evaluation of the opportunity cost of an intervention, that is, comparing the result obtained with the best alternative use of available resources. This analysis allows not only for the assessment of whether an intervention is capable of being efficient and effective in itself, but also for consideration of the allocative efficiency of resources. CBA is one of the most applied economic analyses, often used as a tool in environmental and transport policy while CEA is the dominant method for evaluations of healthcare programs.

Once a project/solution is selected, different procurement and contractual solutions are available to deliver it.

When availability-based PPP contracts were introduced in the UK, within the New Public Management agenda, the main objective for authorities was to achieve affordability and value for money (OECD 2008). To support the decision to prefer a PPP solution rather than a standard procurement contract, a specific analysis was introduced, under the term of Value for Money Analysis (VfMA), based on the comparison between the costs faced by a procuring authority associated with these two contractual options. Practically, VfMA computes the present value of the total whole-of-life costs incurred by government for considered alternatives (Burger and Hawkesworth 2011). Differently from economic evaluation frameworks, which inherently incorporate public value dimensions, the VfMA focuses on operational efficiency and effectiveness, rather than on social welfare. In other terms, in its traditional form, it does not consider the impact on society generated by a procurement/contractual solution. Indeed, if an infrastructure is delivered on time, it is not only a matter of cost savings for the authority, but also about delivery of the social benefits associated with the project. Further, in its traditional form, the VfMA assumes that the outputs/results that can be achieved under the two alternative options are the same. When well-conceived, a PPP contract could allow for the achievement of complex goals that the authority would not be able to achieve under a standard procurement contract. This is the inherent nature of a PPP contract. Based on these considerations, it is salient for the authorities not to follow uncritically the UK-based approach to VfMA but to define a methodological approach suitable for measuring the value generated by a PPP contract vis-à-vis a traditional one. The approach should be consistent with the goals to be achieved and it is important not to conduct the VfMA just as a mere theoretical exercise or with a biased approach (i.e. to craft it with the goal to get a positive result from it, in favor of the decision to go with a PPP). The consequence of such a flawed approach would expose the authority to the risk of designing and implementing the subsequent PPP contract without incorporating the level of risk transfer or incentives forecasted in the VfMA itself.

In this chapter, we explain the fundamental principles underpinning the traditional VfMA, which, if conducted rigorously, still represent a valuable approach. Finally we discuss how to incorporate the social dimension into it.

8.2 Value for Money Analysis

As written, the most widespread value for money analysis (VfMA) model (which we refer to as standard) at international level is the one devised by the British government for availability-based PPP, which consists in comparing:

1) the cost of the PPP option (i.e. the discounted cost of payments made by the competent authority [CA] to the economic operator [EO]) with
2) the cost of making the same investment through one or more outsourcing contracts (to design, build, and operate; the operations could also be considered when managed through an in-house approach) and traditional public financing (the so-called Public Sector Comparator—raw PSC or "traditional" option).

In order to properly compare the two options, it is important to consider all direct and indirect costs, in particular those related to risk.

One of the biggest hurdles in VfMA is the definition of PSC. In many cases, PSC is purely theoretical. One of the reasons underpinning the use of PPP is the inability of a CA to commit all necessary resources (economic and human), during the whole life of an infrastructure, to guarantee an adequate level of service. Whereas a PPP contract is based on a long-term financial planning, traditional public planning is very dependent on political cycles, thus inherently based on a short-term perspective. For example, a CA usually invests in predictive maintenance of buildings when budget is available and not when needed. Put differently, financially strained CAs usually commit resources only when maintenance interventions become non deferrable. Therefore, it is important when defining PSC not to think in terms of historical costs but in terms of resources needed to deliver the same level of quality of a PPP contract. Another point of caution is optimism bias. The VfMA may be affected by a high degree of subjectivity due to the need to estimate the costs associated with the two options. Often optimism bias is seen in the underestimate of construction and maintenance costs associated to the PSC option. Optimism bias is also generated by cash accounting rules, which, compared to accrual accounting, may not allow all costs related to a service/infrastructure to be taken into consideration.

Further, the value of risks transferred or retained under the two approaches represents the "devil" of such analysis. Under the traditional approach, the CA retains some risks that are borne by the EO in a PPP contract. Retaining risks has a cost and it must be accounted for in the comparison. For example, the value of risks retained under the PSC option could be over-estimated in order to prioritize the PPP solution; on the contrary, risks retained can be underestimated for optimism bias. Risks retained or transferred are also difficult to estimate due to a lack of data, especially for operations.

Another evaluation problem is generated by the so-called competitive neutrality, included in the standard VfMA. It takes into account the different taxation profiles underpinning the two options. Indeed, a PPP contract may generate extra tax-revenues for the government vis-à-vis those generated by standard outsourcing contracts. However, extra tax-revenues are cashed in by the central government and rarely by the CA; this may cause unexpected cost for the latter during the execution of the contract.

In general, the standard VfMA is adequate in cases of purely infrastructure investments, while it may be less relevant in contracts where the service component is dominant or where an investment leads to major change in the delivery of a public service. Such changes are possible only if the service is designed and managed under an incentives-based contract such as a PPP, by EOs. Therefore, when the PPP contract is applied to achieve innovation in the service design and delivery, it would be better to compare the costs and benefits associated with a PPP contract with those associated with the status quo, that is, the costs and benefits associated to the level and type of service delivered by the CA at the moment when the analysis is carried out.

Indeed, the methodology is gradually evolving in order to incorporate the "effectiveness" dimension into the evaluation through the combination of the standard VfMA methodologies with CBA elements [see Sects. 8.5 and 8.6]. When VfMA takes place for tariff-based PPPs, where the tariffs potentially applied in a PPP are compared with those of a traditional approach, it is of paramount importance to eliminate bias in the evaluation and also to consider the different level of innovation that the two contractual solutions may deliver to final users.

8.3 How to Carry Out a Standard Value for Money Analysis

In a nutshell, VfMA consists in comparing the net present value of PSC and PPP. There are two main approaches to calculate the PPP and the PSC options:

- one is based on a "build-up approach" and consists in discounting each cost factor;
- another common approach is based on cash flow statements: one to calculate the availability charge that the EO is most likely to offer within the procurement process (the so-called shadow bid); and one to calculate the net present value of the overall disbursements that the CA would face under the PSC option. As noted by the NAO in the UK (National Audit Office 2013), the calculation of the shadow bid represents a more complex approach, though more realistic, as it normally estimates a PPP cost higher than that calculated through the so-called building-up approach.

Looking at the "build-up approach," the PSC calculation formula is as follows:

$$\sum_{t=1}^{n}\left(\frac{\begin{array}{c} base\,cost_t + competitive\,neutrality_t + financing\,costs_t \\ + transferrable\,risks_t + witheld\,risks_t \end{array}}{(1+i)^t}\right).$$

where:

Base cost (raw PSC)	sum of costs and any expected revenues of the entire life cycle of the project (coinciding with the contract) associated with certain technical-functional specifications and expected service levels
Competitive neutrality	neutralizes any competitive advantages/disadvantages of PSC compared to a PPP linked, for example, to the tax treatment of transactions in the different models (Taxes, VAT)
Financing costs	they are often included in the basic cost, together with the investment, through the determination of a symbolic repayment installment of a loan taken out for the realization of the investment
Risks transferred	value of risks transferred to the private partner under traditional procurement contracts
Withheld risks	value of the risks retained by the PA
i	discount rate
t	duration (comparable to the PPP contract)

The base cost items of the so-called raw PSC are:

- capital investments;
- operating costs;
- operating and maintenance costs;
- disposal costs;
- indirect costs (e.g. administrative costs for carrying out the award procedures).

With reference to financing, there may be two models to choose from:

- debt financing: in this case, a bank loan is added to the cash flows of the PSC option to cover the investment and, during management, the repayment instalment of the loan, together with financial charges.
- pay-as-you-go financing: in this case, it is expected that the investment tranches are covered with the administration's own funds.

The first option may be comparable to the identification of shareholder's cash flows, whereas in the second option we get something similar to project cash flows. In the latter, the capital investment is charged upfront during the construction phases, thus generating an increased value of the discounted cost of the PSC option.

Grants, if any, shall always be deducted from the investment cost both for PSC and PPP.

As discussed in Sect. 8.2, the competitive neutrality should be considered only if the CA retains the extra tax revenues generated by the PPP; the incremental tax revenues generated by a PPP should be considered as a cost in the PSC, in other words they represent a loss in revenues in the case of a traditional option.

An important element of the calculation of the VfMA is the selection of the discount rate, to be used for discounting the cash flows under the two options, PPP and PSC. Indeed, the VfMA is the difference between the discounted cost of PPP and the discounted cost of PSC. In the UK, HM Treasury applies the social time preference rate, which reflects social attitudes to spending now as opposed to the future. Since this rate is above the cost of public borrowing, the UK model arguably understates the additional cost of using private finance compared to government borrowing (National Audit Office 2013). In British Columbia, in contrast, the discount rate applied is the IRR of the shadow bid and, for this reason, the approach has been criticized as it clearly overestimates the cost of the PSC option. In Ontario, France, and Italy, the discount rate applied is the cost of public borrowing. If the VfMA is adopted as a mere financial analysis, for the assessment of availability of PPP contracts vis-à-vis a standard approach and without considering social benefits, the use of the cost of public borrowing seems the most appropriate; as a matter of fact, the analysis is based on the comparison of cash flows generated by the options for the CAs.

Looking at PPP, its base cost is represented by the net present value of the availability charges paid by the CA, to be calculated as the remuneration, for the EO, of the following costs:

- design costs;
- capitalized investment costs;
- financial charges;
- maintenance/operation costs;
- the return on the risk capital (equity) invested.

This analysis is simpler in the context of an unsolicited proposal since the CA can use the availability charges and other fees proposed by the solicitor. In the case of solicitation by the CA, a financial plan must be prepared to calculate the shadow bid to be paid to the EO. Often, however, this financial plan is produced on the basis of historical data from the CA and therefore the VfMA does not allow any real consideration of the value that can be generated under a PPP option. The consequence of such an approach is that the PPP may result in being more expensive, because the only differential factor is the cost of public and private capitals, especially when risks are difficult to estimate due to a lack of data.

If the VfMA also aims at taking project outcomes into consideration, the evaluator shall identify positive/negative impact, and translate it into monetary terms, bearing in mind that, in a traditional approach, the risk for failing to reach the desired outcome is always borne by the CA, whereas a PPP contract can enforce the achievement of such results. To include this kind of assessment in the VfMA it is necessary, of course, to have sound data, which can be quite difficult and costly. A possible stylized approach is described in Sect. 8.6.

One of the most critical elements in the VfMA is certainly the definition of the risks retained by the CA under PSC. Risk assessment should take into account all types of risk, as defined in the project risk matrix, and their impact. The difficulty derives from the fact that analytical accounting tools are rarely used, therefore there is no historical data to rely on for estimating the cost of such risks.

A quantification of the retained risks could be made starting from data referring to a sample of projects similar to the one being evaluated (managed in a traditional way) by trying to isolate those higher costs associated with responsibilities that in a PPP contract would be transferred to the EO (and thereby identifying the net risks retained by the CA). The choice of data and comparison projects is essential for the validity of the analysis.

The financial quantification of each risk may differ depending on whether it is transferred to the EO or it is retained by the CA according on their relative ability to manage efficiently and effectively those risks they are responsible for. An EO, for example, may be more effective at managing technical risks compared to the CA because it is better equipped at devoting resources to anticipate and mitigate risk occurrence in order to avoid related negative impacts.

Generally, it is easier to assess risks during the construction phase, such as higher costs and longer times; much more complex, however, is the evaluation of those under management, for the reasons explained in Sect. 8.2.

Where it is not possible to use a quantitative risk assessment, a qualitative assessment may be sufficient, paying attention to the main contractual clauses of the PPP and comparing them with those used in a traditional delivery approach.

Section 8.4 presents an example useful for understanding how to apply a standard VfMA for a large infrastructure project.

8.4 The VfMA of a PPP Contract for a Large Hospital in North Africa

Here we present a real case to show how a robust VfMA can be performed in a context characterized by a lack of sound data. The case is also useful to understand how a PPP contract can be designed in order to make it consistent with the specific features of the context.

The VfMA was carried out to assess the convenience of a PPP solution, compared to a standard public procurement, to design, build, finance, and maintain a new university hospital (NUH) in a large city in North Africa. The population is covered by social health insurance (SHI). Indigent people not covered by SHI are covered by the Ministry of Health (MoH). Healthcare services are mainly delivered by public hospitals, but they have very low hospital occupancy rates, frequent drug stock-outs (especially in rural facilities), and equipment breakdowns and shortages. In recent years, several private hospitals opened, though subsidized by the central government, and this generated a migration of clinicians from public to private hospitals. Large university hospitals and specialized hospital facilities (i.e. those likely to be suitable for the PPP approach) are managed at the central level, others by powerful autonomous directorates. Budgets for investments are separated from those for operational expenditure. Hence, integrated planning of capital and maintenance costs is severely hampered. Capital spending nationally, taking into account private spending, accounts for only a thin slice (less than 10%) of total health spending.

The NUH was part of a major investment plan launched in 2014. An international call for proposals was launched and the offer made by a consortium formed by some international renown players was chosen to develop the project. A subsequent deterioration of the macroeconomic scenario put on hold the project which never saw the light of day.

The VfMA followed a detailed analysis aimed at choosing the most appropriate PPP model for the goals to be achieved and the context. The model chosen was a DBFM/light PPP contract (see Chap. 4).

The DBFM appeared more appropriate for the following reasons:

1. it was easier to structure and develop, as it focused only on design, finance, and maintenance for the NHU facilities and did not include ancillary/soft services or clinical activities;
2. it was coherent, with the main goal the provision of an NUH (i.e. to increase the public health system's quality and capacity, thanks to

the opportunity to offer better clinical services) thus offsetting the expansion of the private sector and retaining clinical personnel in the public health system;

3. by not including the ancillary/soft services, which can be outsourced through short-term contracts, it was more flexible, thus reducing transaction costs and securing a better value for money overall; this would have also made the project more socially acceptable, since many ancillary services are in-house managed by public employees.

However, to make the DBFM model more adequate to deliver a fully functioning hospital, medical equipment should be included in the perimeter of the contract, through a ring-fenced Managed Equipment Service (MES) contract which would be part of the DBFM but separately managed by specialized operators. An MES contract is a specific form of PPP for the provision and management of medical equipment. This solution is optimal to increase the value for money of the medical component, which is more sensitive than facilities to obsolescence and requires a direct and not intermediated relationship between the hospital and the MES operator. Further, two strains of payments were designed: one for the hospital facilities and maintenance and one for the MES, thus ensuring more efficient allocation of margins between the SPV (and therefore the Energy Performance Contractor) and the medical equipment provider, thus reducing the risk that the former may retain margins at the expense of resources and incentives for the latter, and therefore ensuring an adequate flow of money to provide the necessary quality in the management and renewal of the medical equipment.

That said the options under evaluation were the following (as summarized in Fig. 8.1):

- **PSC**: a public procurement works contract for the construction of the new hospital building coupled with separate procurements for the supply of medical equipment and their maintenance and for the maintenance services;
- **PPP option 1**: a 30-year DBFM contract enclosing a 16-year MES contract;
- **PPP option 2**: a 30-year DBFM contract, with the option of a lump-sum payment at the end of the construction phase to repay up to the 80% of the construction cost, enclosing a 16-year MES contract, in the event that macroeconomic conditions improved.

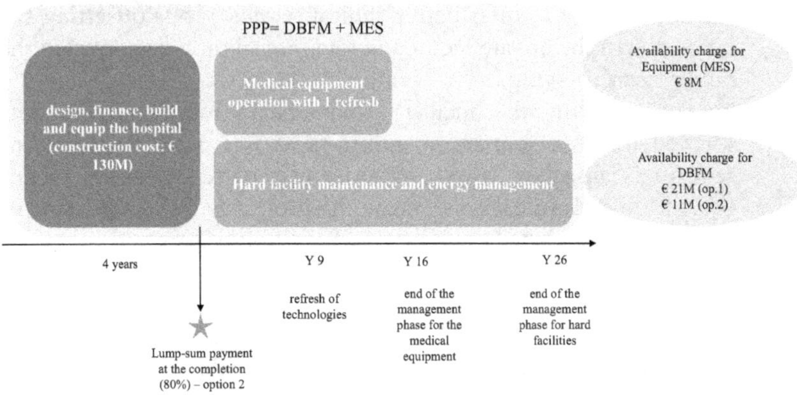

Fig. 8.1 Structure of the PPP contract designed

Table 8.1 Statistical analysis results to prepare construction risks scenarios

	Construction risk (% of increase in costs)	*Construction risk (number of days of delays)*
Number of observations	30	26
Skewness	3089	0.590
Kurtosis	10,118	-0.455
Average	20.72%	66%
StDev	9%	55%
Median	17.6%	0.6
Min	0.0%	0%
Max	119.5%	180%

8.4.1 The Evaluation Process

The assessment was carried out in three steps:

1. data collection to estimate input data and risks, both for PSC and PPP;
2. preparation of the financial plan to calculate cash flow associated with the PSC and the PPP options (calculation of the shadow bid, i.e. the availability charges for options 1 and 2);
3. VfM analysis.

To estimate the costs associated with the PSC option, country-specific data were collected. To estimate costs associated to the PPP option and the value of risks retained/transferred, data of comparable projects were collected in Europe and the Mediterranean region. Overall, 38 comparable initiatives were analyzed. Here the weakness stands in the use of international data to compute for the value of risks in PSC; however, it was the only possible approach, considering the lack of traditional projects data in that country. However, considering the institutional context, with a lack of specialized skills in the public sector, the results of the analysis can be considered conservative and the impact of retained risks under the PSC option could be greater.

To calculate the cost associated with the PSC, these assumptions were considered:

- an inflation rate of 4% to be applied to the investment costs each year.
- the equipment renewal happens with a delay of 4 years vis-à-vis the schedule included in the PPP. For this reason, it could be considered as an increase in maintenance costs of 10% to 15% during such a period;
- the investment is paid according to the "pay-as-you-go" mechanism;
- since the project is funded by the central government, competitive neutrality was also included.

A statistical analysis was used to calculate the cost associated with construction risk (measured by cost increases and delays) retained by the government under the PSC option. Risks during the operational phase were not considered in the analysis due to a lack of reliable data. Data were normalized and plotted in a Q-Q plot to verify if risks followed a normal distribution or not. The results showed that this was the case for extra-budget risk, but not exactly for extra-time because of a more skewed distribution with fatter tails.

To calculate the value of construction risks retained under the PSC, two different approaches were used, one to compute the costs overrun and one for the delay, in order to consider their impacts correctly.

Overall, three scenarios were performed, the best case, the worst case, and the average—based respectively on the minimum, maximum, and average impact of risks. Therefore, for the risk of costs overruns, minimum, average, and maximum values were used to calculate the increase in the construction cost in each scenario.

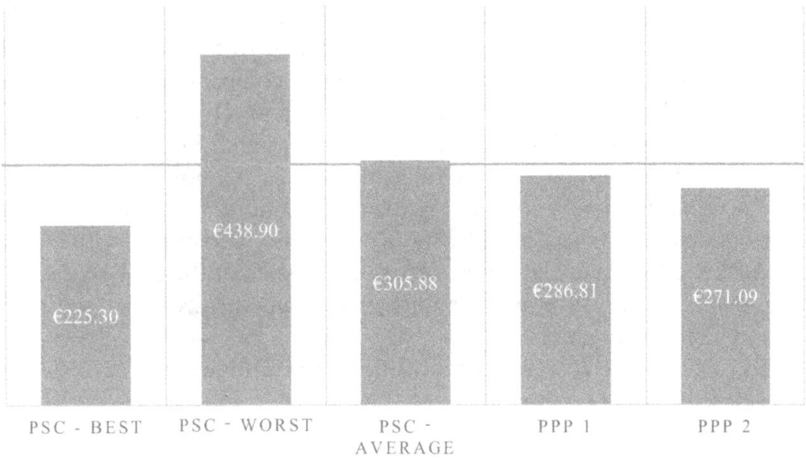

Fig. 8.2 Comparison of net NPV in EUR millions adjusted for risk of cost overruns

The results of the assessment are presented in Fig. 8.2. As we may see the risk-adjusted net present value (NPV) of PPP options is lower than three different PSC scenarios.

In order to assess the robustness of the analysis, the average value and standard deviation of NPV of different PSC scenarios were calculated and 10,000 estimates of values assumed by the PSC under a normal and log-normal distribution of risk probabilities were sampled randomly. This allowed to state that there's a 60%-70% chance that the PPP could be cheaper than PSC.

To calculate the risk of delay, a straightforward approach in the healthcare sector is to look at lost clinical production as measured by tariffs (such as DRGs). This approach was not possible in the country where the project is located, because DRGs did not exist at the time of evaluation. Indeed, extending the length of the construction phase in the PSC option would generate a reduction in the NPV, in favor of the PSC, as a consequence of the time value of money.

Therefore, the social rate of time preference was applied to the cost of construction, considering different scenarios of delay (minimum, average, and maximum). The social rate of time preference applied is the cost of government capital, as suggested by many authors and used in valuation practice (EPEC 2011).

Despite the fact that the VfMA does not consider the risks retained by the government in the PSC scenario, results are sufficiently strong to support the decision to prefer a PPP contract. It is important to reiterate that the allocation of risk estimated in the VfMA should be incorporated in the PPP contract, with a sound system of deductions/penalties, in order to achieve the forecasted value for money.

8.5 Value for Money: How to Include the Social Dimension in the Analysis of Infrastructure PPP Projects[1]

As discussed in Sect. 1.2, a necessary innovation to be introduced in the VfMA is the dimension of social impact. In fact, the PPP allows for objectives that are often unachievable for CAs and not only for financial reasons (lack of sufficient budget to build a complex project in a reasonable period in order to quickly answer to a certain social need) but also for operational ones. This approach is based on the public value framework analyzed in Chap. 1.

To do this, simplified CBA elements can be incorporated in the standard VfMA. Here, we present a case (the construction of a bypass) to understand how to carry out such an evaluation. In particular, the case incorporates in the VfMA the social loss generated by the construction delay. Differently from the case used in Sect. 8.4, which was performed to support the real decision to implement a PPP project; here, the case is prepared with a purely theoretical/explanatory goal, to show, ex post, the benefit that a PPP solution would have generated. Actually, the object of their analysis was implemented through a standard DB contract and not a PPP. Delays and costs overruns which were experienced could be used to estimate the costs of risks associated to a PSC option. Therefore, risks are not estimated by using a statistical approach, because real ex post data are available.

Since the hypothetical project is a bypass, the analysis does not consider social benefits generated by a different model of service delivery, which may be present when taking into consideration other possible fields of PPP application.

In 2010, a CA awarded the tender for the DB of a road of approximately 6 km. The executive design started in January 2011 and the works in August of the same year. During the realization of the works, various technical and operational problems caused delays and required changes in

[1] This case was elaborated with the support of Erika Avanzi, who developed the analysis as part of her final thesis within the SDA Bocconi Executive Master in Public Management.

the project. In particular, the works uncovered a waste dump in the subsoil and, given the particular chemical nature of the excavation soil, this implied the need to modify the route, with further expropriation costs. Additional costs were also associated with the displacement of technological lines interfering with the construction site due to the discovery of plants not initially mapped in a very large area.

Under a PPP contract, these extra costs would have been transferred to the OE, who would have had the contractual and financial incentives to avoid them, under penalty of non-recovery of the investment made. In addition, the serious financial situation of the construction company, chosen as per a traditional selection approach based on the lowest price, caused a further delay. The works ended in October 2015, after a total duration of 53 months as opposed to the 22 initially planned.

Overall, the project costed about €30 million instead of the estimated €24.3 million plus VAT. Of this figure, in a PPP scheme, €8.2 million could have been considered the responsibility of the private partner, which, unlike the DB contractor, could have put in place all the activities aimed at avoiding extra costs and extra time.

Negative externalities, generated by execution delays, which forced users to lengthen their daily commute, must also be added to the overall costs. To this end, only the costs incurred by the community for the time lost (about 20 minutes each way) traveling on the existing state road instead of the new faster-running bypass during the additional 29 months of delay were considered.

Traffic surveys on the existing highway recorded an average of 8485 vehicles in transit every day. To calculate the value of this social cost, the average income of the county where the road is located was taken into consideration and the average net income per capita per day was calculated, which was equal to €75.45p/day. Considering, on average, a loss of 20 minutes for 220 working days a year, the overall cost faced by the community was about €14 million, as shown in Table 8.2.

To understand whether the PPP would have been more convenient, the hypothetical availability charge (gross of VAT, which represents a non-recovered cost for the CA) was calculated for the definition of the hypothetical total cost of the PPP contract. The availability charge was calculated on the basis of the original cost of the investment and is equal to €50.6 million.

The net present value of the PSC was defined also considering maintenance costs and the extra costs actually recorded in the DB contract. The latter represents associated costs of construction risk. Overall, it amounts

Table 8.2 The calculation of negative externalities for the local community

Number of vehicles per day	*8485*
Average daily net income (€)	75.45
Average net income per minute (8h/day)	0.16
Delay per vehicle (minutes)	20
Working days per year	220
Working days per month	18.3
Months of delay	29
Economic cost of externality (€/month)	489,036.51
Total economic cost of externality (€)	**14,182,058.80**

Table 8.3 Value for money with the inclusion of the social benefit (in €)

PSC (construction and maintenance)	*35,966,671.97*
Extra costs associated to DB contract	5,700,000.00
Total PSC with extra financial costs	**41,666,671.97**
Social cost for the delay	14,182,058.80
Total PSC cost including the delay	55,848,730.77
PPP	50,604,682.13
VfM	**5,244,048.64**

to €41.6 million. To make the analysis more conservative, no risk was accounted for the management phase.

Without considering the negative social externality, the PPP is more expensive than the traditional model by about €9 million. This extra cost is mainly due to higher financing costs and negative tax effects (the competitive neutrality was not considered).

Considering the social costs, valued at approximately €14 million, it is possible to state that the PPP would have generated a total value of approximately €5.2 million and an extra tax revenue for the Revenue Agency of approximately €8 million euros overall. It should be considered that the former is an economic and not a financial value, which has no impact on the public sector budget. This example is useful for showing how a contract can generate social loss or benefit and why CBA elements should be included in the VfMA.

Therefore, in addition to the results shown in Table 8.2, the impact of delay risk should be considered (looking at cost overruns), which was calculated in the range from €94 million (7 years of delays—worst scenario) to €43 million in the average scenario (2 years of delays).

8.6 Value for Money: How to Include the Social Dimension in the Analysis of PPP Projects Based on a Service Innovation

An analysis of the social costs generated by a traditional public delivery mode can also be useful to structure PPP contracts with a scheme of incentives to tackle associated social issues.

In this case, there is no need to use a traditional VfMA because the CA has to compare two delivery modalities: a traditional model vis-à-vis an outcome-based PPP contract, where the former would not achieve the same level of social performance due to its inherent nature (i.e. the lack of a payment linked to certain social performance indicators).

The methodological approach can be summarized in Fig. 8.3.

To understand the achievable positive impacts with an outcome-based PPP, we can refer to the case of so-called urban facility management (hereafter UFM) as a form of integrated management of support services for the operation, use, and enhancement of urban assets (depending on the specific needs, it may include maintenance of the road network,

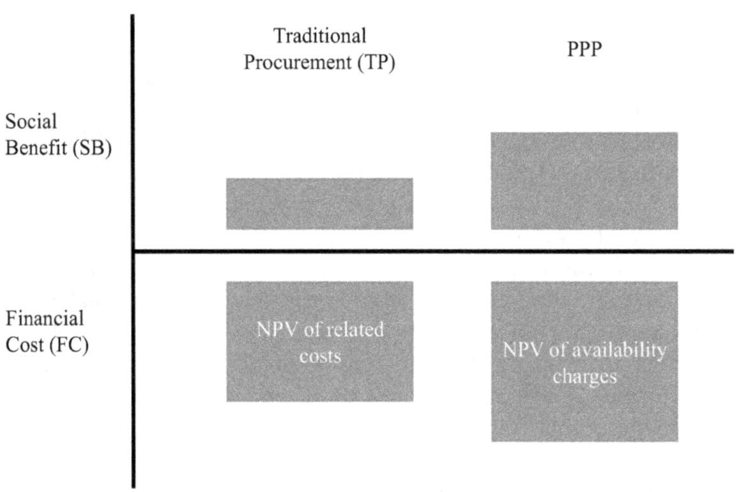

VFM_{PPP} when : $FC_{TP} - SB_{TP} > FC_{PPP} - SB_{PPP}$

Fig. 8.3 A scheme of the VfMA applied to outcome-based PPPs

management and cleaning of greenery, maintenance and control of technological underground utilities, maintenance of street furniture).

In the case of a PPP, an EO would be in charge of coordinating these services that are usually scattered across several departments in the municipality, agencies, and public utility companies. This scattering may hamper the efforts to tackle negative externalities linked to the use of road: traffic congestion, pollution, noise, road accidents.

To better understand the social costs of such externalities, that is, the potential benefits of changing the way public spaces are managed, we carried out a simulation on a mid-dimension city in South Europe by using the methodology developed by the European Commission (European Commission 2019; Korzhenevych et al. 2014).

The urban area has a population of about 400,000 inhabitants, with an average of 2000 accidents per year, 25 deaths and 2500 injuries. The social cost of these events amounts to approximately €132 million for the community. The cost of polluting emissions from transport in this urban area amounts to about €42 million. Cost related to climate change could be worth €27.8 million. Noise pollution has a cost in a range between €24.4 and €50.4 million. The cost of congestion is the most difficult to calculate because of the lack of data. However, it can be assumed that it is in a range between 333 million and €1.3 billion. Summing these data, we can estimate that urban traffic has an annual social cost of between 1.4% and 4.02% of the city GDP.

The municipality already has a contract in place for the management of some UFM services, of about €14 million per year (including management of signs, snow, and road maintenance work). The total expenditure that can be deduced from the analytical accounting, including personnel costs, for items referable to road management indicates a cost of about €75 million incurred in 2018 alone.

Assuming that a more effective management of these services through a PPP contract, which can create effective incentives for the EO to achieve at least a 1% reduction in externalities, would compensate greatly for an increase in the budget dedicated to these services (assuming that the PPP would cost more than a traditional delivery mode).

Such an analysis can be useful to calculate the potential reduction in social costs that could compensate for a hypothetical budget increase, due to the choice of implementing an outcome-based PPP. Further, it is helpful to set realistic targets for social outcomes, to be linked to a system of deductions, to be achieved by the EOs (as discussed Chap. 4). This example is also useful to understand possible application of social impact bond (SIB) schemes, described in Chap. 6, to a new set of services, thus expanding the application of SIB from social to societal services, that is, services for the benefit of larger communities.

References

Burger, P., & Hawkesworth, I. (2011). How To Attain Value for Money : Comparing PPP and Traditional Infrastructure Public Procurement by. *OECD Journal on Budgeting, 2011*(1), 1–56. https://doi.org/10.1787/16812336.

Drummond, M. F., Sculpher, M. J., Claxton, K., Stoddart, G. L., & Torrance, G. W. (2015). *Methods for the Economic Evaluation of Health Care Programmes.* Oxford: Oxford University Press.

EPEC. (2011). *The Non-Financial Benefits of PPPs A Review of Concepts and Methodology.*

European Commission. (2019). *Handbook on External Costs of Transport.* https://doi.org/10.2832/27212

Korzhenevych, A., Dehnen, N., Bröcker, J., Holtkamp, M., Meier, H., Gibson, G., Varna, A., & Cox, V. (2014). Update of the Handbook on External Costs of Transport. *Final Report, 1*, 139. https://doi.org/Ref: ED 57769—Issue Number 1

National Audit Office. (2013). *Review of the VFM Assessment Process for PFI. October.*

OECD. (2008). *Public-Private Partnerships in Pursuit of Risk Sharing and Value for Money.*

Index[1]

[1] Note: Page numbers followed by 'n' refer to notes.

V. Vecchi et al., *Public Private Partnerships*,
https://doi.org/10.1007/978-3-030-65435-1

CPSIA information can be obtained
at www.ICGtesting.com
Printed in the USA
LVHW080842100521
686961LV00004B/424